United States
of America

5. Carefully apply a thin stripe of white nail polish to the tip of a nail. Follow the natural line of the white part. When you are finished, the line should look like an upside-down smiley face.

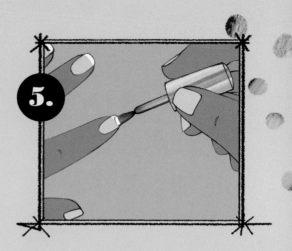

6. If your line is too thick or uneven, wet the end of a Q-tip with a tiny amount of nail polish remover. Run the Q-tip under the smiley face to make the line smoother or thinner.

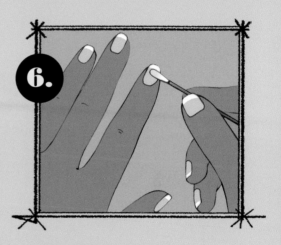

7. Repeat on the rest of your nails on that hand.

8. Wait carefully for your polish to dry. Don't type, open doors, or touch anything, including your phone, for at least ten minutes.

9. For a second coat of polish to give your nails a brighter look, repeat steps 5 to 8.

10. Tap the polish lightly at one corner of a nail. If it is hard, you can repeat steps 5 to 8 for the nails on the other hand. If you added a second coat on the first hand, add one to the nails on this hand too. Your manicure will look fabulous!

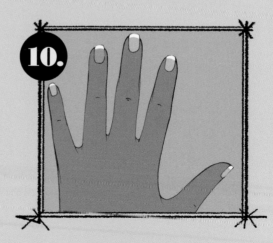

United States
of America

BY MARTIN HINTZ

Enchantment of the World
Second Series

Children's Press®

A Division of Scholastic Inc.

NEW YORK   TORONTO   LONDON   AUCKLAND   SYDNEY
MEXICO CITY   NEW DELHI   HONG KONG
DANBURY, CONNECTICUT

Frontispiece: America's heartland

Consultant: Robert D. Johnston, Associate Professor of History, Yale University, New Haven, CT

Please note: All statistics are as up-to-date as possible at the time of publication.

Book production by Herman Adler Design

Library of Congress Cataloging-in-Publication Data

Hintz, Martin.
   United States of America / by Martin Hintz
         p. cm. — (Enchantment of the world. Second series)
Includes bibliographical references and index.
ISBN 0-516-24246-6
1. United States—Juvenile literature. [1. United States.] I. Title. II. Series
E156.H56 2003
973—dc21   2002156743

CHILDREN'S PRESS and associated logos are trademarks and or registered trademarks of Scholastic Library Publishing. SCHOLASTIC and associated logos are trademarks and or registered trademarks of Scholastic Inc.
1 2 3 4 5 6 7 8 9 10 R 13 12 11 10 09 08 07 06 05 04

Acknowledgments

The author wishes to thank those who helped in writing Enchantment of the World *United States of America*. Special appreciation goes to the educators, librarians, and others who reviewed the manuscript and offered their suggestions, especially Brenda Fay, children's librarian, North Shore Library, Glendale, Wisconsin, and my wife, Pam Percy. Special appreciation also must go to all those long-distant ancestors who took a chance, left the Old World, and came to the United States to start a new life.

To all the children of September 11, 2001, wherever they live.

Cover photo:
Fireworks display over the Capital Building in Washington, D.C.

Contents

Alaskan landscape

Lincoln Memorial

CHAPTER ONE

Introducing the United States

To much of the world, the United States of America is an example of freedom and democracy. It is a country to be emulated, or copied, in many ways. The sense that power belongs to the people, and that government must answer to its people, is at the root of the American system of law. While many Americans take for granted the freedoms guaranteed by their democratic system of government, these freedoms are just far-away dreams for people of some other countries.

The U.S. Constitution is the world's oldest document in continuous use. It presents the fundamental laws of the United States. Other nations regularly adopt the lofty principles found in the Constitution for their own use. The United States has a long history of supporting democratic principles around the world. It stands tall as the world's lone military superpower. With this power comes responsibility. The United States cannot stand alone. The world is much too small. It takes wise leaders and wise citizens to realize this and to encourage, as well as to support, cooperation between nations. This can be a hard job, but for more than 200 years, leaders of the United States have been trying to do just that. While the fit may not always be perfect, Americans are still proud that they are generally respected for their system of government.

The American media sets the trend for global pop culture. Young people around the world love American movies,

Opposite: **Drafted by the Constitutional Congress Convention in Philadelphia, Pennsylvania, in 1787, the Constitution is the fundamental law of the United States.**

American dance steps, and American music. International teens copy American clothing styles, slang, and eating habits.

Not all people like the United States. Some think that the American government is too pushy and self-centered when dealing with other countries. They feel that some American leaders do not listen to them or understand their problems. Others dislike the United States because they feel that the spread of American culture upsets their traditional way of doing things.

Over the past 200 years, however, the image of freedom found in the United States has been powerful enough to attract millions of newcomers from all corners of the earth. Many of them braved terrible hardships to reach the shores of the United States. Eager for a new life, most came with only what they could carry. Some arrivals sought political freedom. Others believed that the streets would be paved with gold. Immigrants spread throughout the land, passing on their vision of what makes a wonderful life to their descendants. From the country's very beginning, immigrants felt that the United States was infinitely better than what they had left behind in the Old World.

Many people emigrated to the United States in hopes of bettering their economic and personal well being.

There is no typical American. Originating from a multitude of ethnic backgrounds, Americans come in all shapes, sizes, colors, and ages. They practice a rainbow of religions and have a variety of political beliefs. They are doctors, nurses, scientists, plumbers, teachers, pilots, cowboys, and salespeople. Some Americans do not have jobs, but other Americans try to help them.

Americans live in mansions, small houses, and apartments. They live in sprawling cities, reservations, trim suburbs, farms, and villages. Sadly, many are homeless. Some families can trace their American roots back for generations; others have just arrived. The population is growing more diverse all the time. This broad mix of races and heritages makes a wonderful blend of energy, talent, and creativity. For good reason, the country's motto is *E pluribus unum:* From many, one.

The United States population is a "melting pot" made up of people from many ethnic and cultural backgrounds.

**Geopolitical map of the
United States**

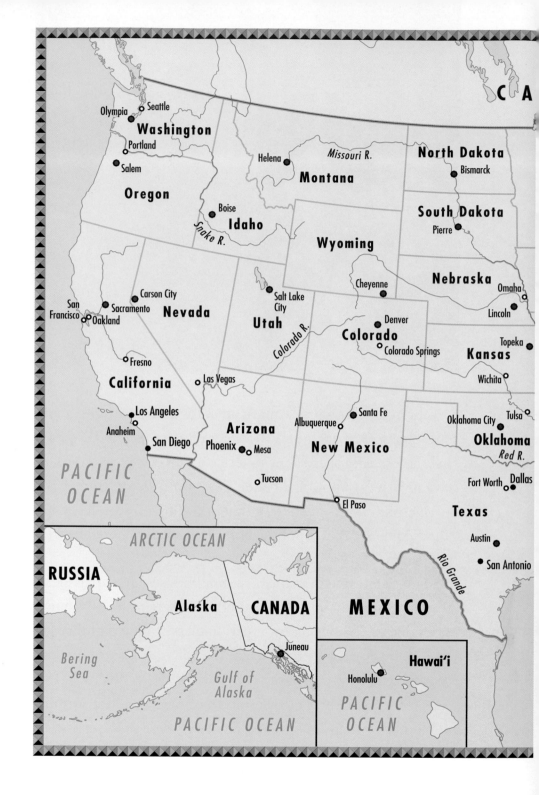

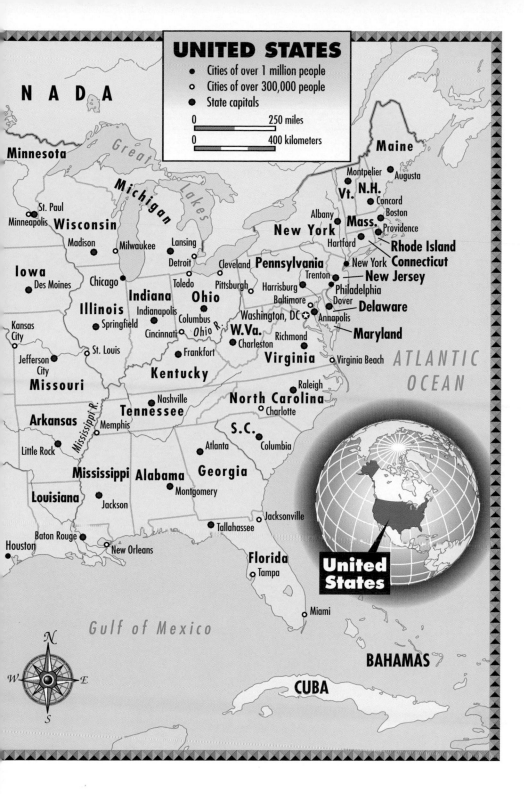

UNITED STATES

- • Cities of over 1 million people
- ○ Cities of over 300,000 people
- • State capitals

0 ———— 250 miles

0 ———— 400 kilometers

N A D A

Minnesota

Great Lakes

Michigan

Maine

Montpelier Augusta

Vt. N.H.

Concord

St. Paul

Minneapolis Wisconsin

Madison Milwaukee Lansing

Albany Boston

Mass.

Providence

Hartford Rhode Island

New York

Detroit

Cleveland Pennsylvania

New York Connecticut

Iowa

Des Moines Chicago

Toledo

Pittsburgh

Trenton New Jersey

Indiana Ohio

Harrisburg Philadelphia

Illinois Indianapolis

Columbus

Baltimore Dover Delaware

Kansas City

Springfield

Cincinnati Ohio R.

Washington, DC Annapolis

St. Louis

W.Va.

Richmond Maryland

Jefferson City

Frankfort

Charleston

Missouri Kentucky

Virginia Virginia Beach

ATLANTIC OCEAN

Raleigh

Nashville North Carolina

Arkansas Tennessee

Charlotte

Memphis

S.C.

Little Rock

Atlanta Columbia

Mississippi Alabama Georgia

Louisiana Jackson Montgomery

Jacksonville

Baton Rouge Tallahassee

Houston New Orleans

Florida

Tampa

Gulf of Mexico

Miami

United States

BAHAMAS

CUBA

N
W E
S

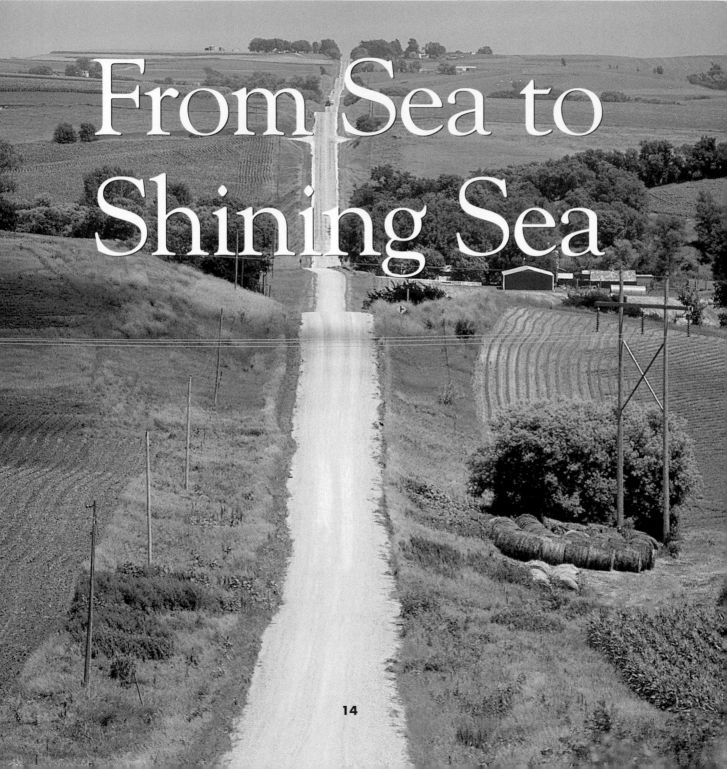

From Sea to Shining Sea

THE CONTINENTAL UNITED STATES IS EASY TO FIND. IT IS located between Canada to the north and Mexico to the south, the Atlantic Ocean to the east, and the Pacific Ocean to the west. Many international visitors are surprised at the size of the country. Some travelers think they can spend a couple of days in New York, then spend a few hours driving to Chicago before heading out to see the Rocky Mountains that same afternoon. They quickly learn the real story.

The United States covers a total area of 4 million square miles (10 million square kilometers). This includes 79,481 square miles (205,856 sq km) of inland water, not counting

Opposite: **As the third largest nation in the world, the United States covers 4 million square miles from coast to coast.**

A satellite image shows the immensity of the continent of North America.

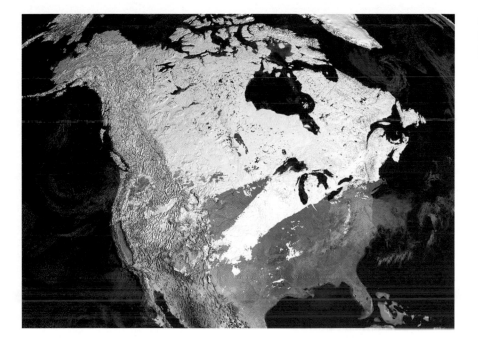

United States Geographical Features

Highest Elevation: Mount McKinley, Alaska, 20,320 feet (6,198 m)

Lowest Elevation: Death Valley, California, 282 feet (86 m) below sea level

Longest River: Mississippi River, 2,340 miles (3,766 km)

Largest Lake: Lake Superior, 350 miles (560 km) long, 160 miles (256 km) wide, and 475 feet (144.75 m) deep

Largest Swamp: Florida Everglades National Park, 1,509,000 acres (610,684 ha)

Coastline (excludes Alaska and Hawai'i): 4,993 miles (8,035 km)

Coldest Temperature: Prospect Creek Camp, Endicott Mountains, Alaska, –80°F (–62°C), January 23, 1971

Hottest Temperature: Death Valley, California, 134°F (56°C), July 10, 1913

Average Precipitation (contiguous states): 7.53 inches (19.1 cm) to 72.1 inches (183.2 cm)

Largest City (2000 est.): New York City, 8,008,278 people

Smallest State Capital City (2000 est.): Montpelier, Vermont, 8,035 people

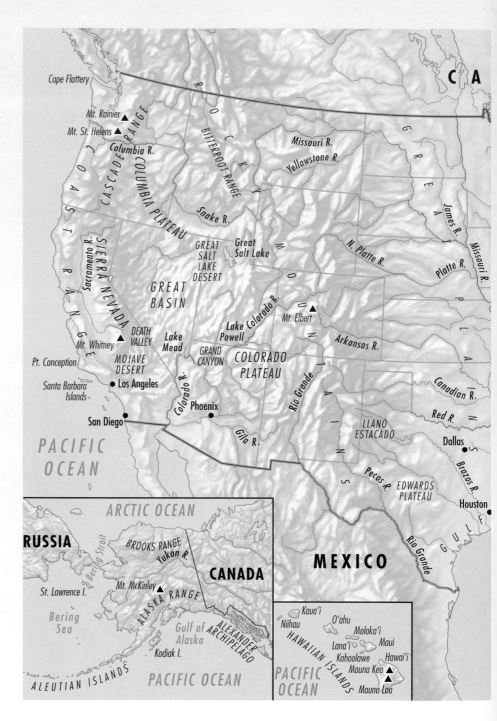

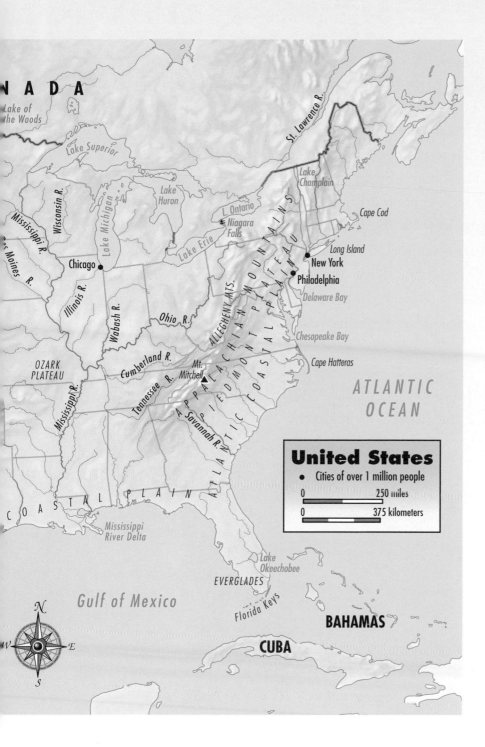

CANADA

Lake of the Woods

Lake Superior

Wisconsin R.

Lake Huron

Lake Michigan

Mississippi R.

Des Moines R.

Chicago

Illinois R.

Wabash R.

Ohio R.

OZARK PLATEAU

Mississippi R.

Cumberland R.

Tennessee R.

Mt. Mitchell

ALLEGHENY MTS.

APPALACHIAN MOUNTAINS

APPALACHIAN PLATEAU

PIEDMONT

Savannah R.

COASTAL PLAIN

ATLANTIC COASTAL PLAIN

St. Lawrence R.

Lake Champlain

L. Ontario

Niagara Falls

Lake Erie

Cape Cod

Long Island

New York

Philadelphia

Delaware Bay

Chesapeake Bay

Cape Hatteras

ATLANTIC OCEAN

COASTAL PLAIN

Mississippi River Delta

Lake Okeechobee

EVERGLADES

Florida Keys

Gulf of Mexico

BAHAMAS

CUBA

United States

● Cities of over 1 million people

0 _____ 250 miles

0 _____ 375 kilometers

N E S W

the Great Lakes, which make up another 94,680 square miles (245,220 sq km). The United States also has 13,942 square miles (36,110 sq km) of coastal waters. Excluding Alaska and Hawai'i, the United States has 4,993 miles (8,035 km) of coastline that includes towering sea cliffs and smooth, sandy beaches.

The United States is the third-largest nation in the world, next in line behind Russia and Canada. The greatest distance east to west on the U.S. mainland is 2,807 miles (4,517 km) and approximately 1,200 miles (1,900 km) from north to south.

Geographers have divided the United States into several distinct regions. First, there are the coastal lowlands along the east coast. They begin in southeastern Maine in New England

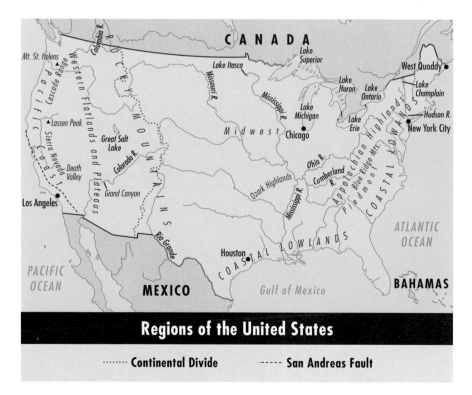

Regions of the United States

········· Continental Divide   ------ San Andreas Fault

Palmetto plants grow along the Cape Canaveral National Seashore in Florida, part of the United States' coastal lowland region.

and extend southward down the coast to Florida's sun-touched beaches and the states along the Gulf of Mexico. These consist of a tip of southern Alabama, plus Mississippi, Louisiana, and eastern Texas. Next inland is the beautifully rugged hills of the Piedmont. The many waterfalls in this region made it difficult for settlers to move inland from the narrow Atlantic coast.

The rugged Piedmont region is located west of the coastal lowlands.

Geographic Extremes

The easternmost point in the United States is the hamlet of West Quoddy, Maine. The northernmost tip of the United States is Alaska's Point Barrow. Alaska also is home to the country's westernmost locale: Cape Wrangell on Attu Island in the far north Pacific. Hawai'i's Ka Lae (South Cape) is the southernmost point of the United States. These far flung locales demonstrate how vast this widespread country really is.

The next region is the Appalachian Highlands. The highlands extend from Maine southwards toward Alabama. This ancient landscape includes the forest-carpeted Blue Ridge Mountains. The Ozark Highlands are located primarily in southern Missouri and northern Arkansas.

Mists created by moisture from the forest rise above lower peaks in the Blue Ridge Mountains.

Long ago the Ojibway Indians called America's longest river Missi Sipi or "Great River."

Fertile Midwestern Plains

The Midwest's fertile plains were flattened eons ago by mile-high glaciers. The Midwest is home to the mighty Mississippi River, the country's longest waterway. The Mississippi stretches 2,340 miles (3,766 km), from its origin out of Lake Itasca in Minnesota to its joining with the Gulf of Mexico.

The sun rises over Big Thompson Creek and distant mountains of the Rockies.

The lofty Rocky Mountains are dramatic snow-capped peaks running from northern Alaska, through Canada, and into northern New Mexico. The Rockies reach as high as 14,000 feet (4,270 meters). The imaginary Continental Divide is found in these mountains. Rivers on one side of this line flow to the east, and those on other side pour downhill to the west.

Death Valley is the hottest and driest place in the United States. Temperatures have reached as high as 134°F (56.7°C).

A dramatic view of Crescent Beach in Oregon and the blue waters of the Pacific Ocean

West of the Rockies lie the dry western flatlands and plateaus. These formations run from eastern Washington, near the Canadian border, and then down to southern California's border with Mexico. While much of the land here is very fertile, it is also the geographic home of parched Death Valley, the lowest place in the United States, lying 282 feet (86 m) below sea level.

The Pacific coast extends southward from western Washington State and Oregon through California. The Cascade and Sierra Nevada Mountains line the eastern edge of this broad area. Active volcanoes, such as California's Lassen Peak and Mount Saint Helens in Washington, still spew smoke and fire. The San Andreas

The Grand Canyon

The Grand Canyon, located in northern Arizona, is one of the most striking natural sites in the world. The canyon itself is 277 miles (446 km) long and varies in width from 4 to about 18 miles (6.4 to 29 km). The average depth is about 1 mile (1.6 km). The fissure was formed by the Colorado River cutting through the landscape some 6 million years ago. Spanish explorers were the first Europeans to see the Grand Canyon, arriving at the gorge in 1540. The Grand Canyon was made into a national park in 1919.

All Shook Up

At 5:12 A.M. on April 18, 1906, an earthquake shook San Francisco, California. The catastrophe caused an estimated half billion dollars and killed more than 3,000 people. The quake lasted only a minute, but it resulted in one of the worst natural disasters in U.S. history. The greatest destruction came from fires that people ignited. Fires ravaged the city for three days before burning themselves out, and 490 city blocks were destroyed. Concerned people in Asia and Europe, as well as Americans throughout the nation, sent aid to help the survivors.

Fault, consisting of plates of rock far under the surface of the earth, is located in this part of the country. Earthquakes result when these plates shift.

North to Alaska

Alaska is tacked on the western side of Canada's Yukon Territory, 500 miles (800 km) north of mainland United States. Almost one-third of Alaska is north of the Arctic Circle, and the summer sun shines up to twenty hours a day. It is dark almost around the clock in the winter. Alaska is the closest part of the United States to Asia. It is only 51 miles (82 km) across the Bering Sea to Siberia's Chukotsk Peninsula in Russia. Alaska is the largest state in the country, covering 663,257 square miles (1,720,000 sq km). This makes it twice the size of Texas, the next-largest state. The greatest distance north to south in Alaska is 1,200 miles (1,930 km); it extends 2,200 miles (3,540 km) east to west. Alaska has the country's highest mountains, as well as most of its active volcanoes.

Alaska, the largest state in the country, offers winding rivers, majestic mountains, and pure wilderness.

Hot Spot Hawai'i

There are 8 major Hawai'ian islands and 114 minor ones. The northernmost island is Kaua'i, which is also called the Garden Island because of its beautiful flowers. Sixty percent of the fiftieth state's population lives on O'ahu, 60 miles (96 km) to the southeast of Kaua'i. To the southeast are Moloka'i, Maui, Lana'i, and Hawai'i.

The Big Island of Hawai'i, the largest in the state's chain, covers 4,021 square miles (10,414 sq km). In fact, the island is still growing. Since 1983, the island has grown by more than 2 billion cubic yards (1.4 billion cubic meters) of land due to volcanic action.

Mountains and coastline along the Na Pali Coast of Kaua'i

Lake Michigan, the only Great Lake that lies entirely within the United States, is 307 miles (494 km) long and 118 miles (189 km) wide.

Each pinprick of rock on the great ocean near Hawai'i is the tip of an ancient mountain. The Hawai'ian islands cover 6,450 square miles (16,729 sq km) and are 2,090 miles (3,364 km) west-southwest of the mainland. The longest distance in Hawai'i is 1,610 miles (2,591 km) from the southeast to the far northwest.

The United States also has territories in the Caribbean Sea and the Pacific Ocean. They include the Commonwealth of Puerto Rico, the Virgin Islands, Guam, and Samoa. The United States also has jurisdiction over several smaller islands, such as tiny Palmyra Island, located about 960 miles (1,536 km) southwest of Honolulu, Hawai'i. Since the conclusion of the Spanish American War in 1898, the United States has controlled a tip of Cuba called Guantanamo Bay.

Abundance of Water

Most of the United States has extensive freshwater supplies, despite occasional droughts. Lakes Ontario, Erie, Huron, Michigan, and Superior make up the Great Lakes. Collectively, the lakes make up one of the world's largest concentrations of quality water. Covering 90,680 square miles (245,220 sq km), the Great Lakes are used for industry, transportation, and recreation. Lake water is also purified for drinking. Water from the Great Salt Lake in Utah is more than five times saltier than the Atlantic Ocean. It covers about 2,500 square miles (6,500 km), with depths ranging from 15 to 80 feet (4.6 to 24 m).

In addition to the Mississippi River, other major rivers in the United States include the Cumberland and the Hudson Rivers in the east, the Missouri and the Ohio Rivers in the Midwest, the Rio Grande in the South, and the Colorado and the Columbia Rivers in the West. There is growing pressure on these river systems due to the country's expanding population. Water is needed for drinking, irrigation, and manufacturing.

Weather Systems

There are many different climates across the United States, although the weather is generally temperate. The city with the most rainfall is Yakutat, Alaska, with 151.25 inches (384.17 centimeters) per year. However, Hilo, Hawai'i, has 278 days of rain compared to Yakutat's 235. Bring mittens and heavy socks to Prospect Creek Camp, nestled in the Endicott Mountains of Alaska, where a record cold of –80° Fahrenheit (–62° Celsius) was recorded on January 23, 1971. Wide-brimmed hats and sunscreen were necessary on July 10, 1913, however, when the country's record heat of 134°F (57°C) occurred in Death Valley, California.

A Look at United States Cities

The rich cultural diversity of the United States is obvious by touring its cities. The largest urban area in the country is New York City, with a total population of 8,008,278 people. Its average temperatures are 31.8°F (0.1°C) in January and 76.1°F (24.5°) in July. Tourists love coming to New York City for its many landmarks, ranging from Broadway theaters to the bright lights of Times Square (below), the Statue of Liberty, and the Empire State Building. New York is the country's artistic and business center. Explorer Giovanni da Varrazano was reportedly the first European to sail into what is now New York Harbor in 1524. Varrazano was followed by Henry Hudson, an Englishman hired by the Dutch. In 1609, Hudson gave his name to the major river that flows past the city.

Los Angeles, California, is the second-largest city, with a population of 3,694,820 people. The city's sprawling neighborhoods are linked by miles of

always-crowded freeways. Downtown Los Angeles's architectural landmarks include City Hall, the Central Library, the Music Center, and the Museum of Contemporary Art. Originally a Spanish mission named in honor of Our Lady, Queen of the Angels, Los Angeles was founded in 1781. It is now known best as the heart of the country's movie-making industry.

Chicago, Illinois, has a population of 2,896,016 people. The city's average temperatures are 22°F (–5.6°C) in January and 74°F (23.3°C) in July. Chicago earned the nickname "Windy City" because of its location on the blustery southwestern shore of

Lake Michigan. Among its many landmarks are the Sears Tower, the Art Institute of Chicago, the bustling Loop business district, and Grant Park (above).

Houston, Texas, has a population of 1,953,63 people. Named after General Sam Houston, a Texas hero, the city was founded in 1836. A center for the petroleum and medical industries, Houston's towering office buildings soar above the flat Texas plains. For fun, locals flock to the Theater District for artistic entertainment and to Reliant Stadium for sporting events. Its average temperatures range from 61°F (16°C) in January to 93°F (35°C) in July.

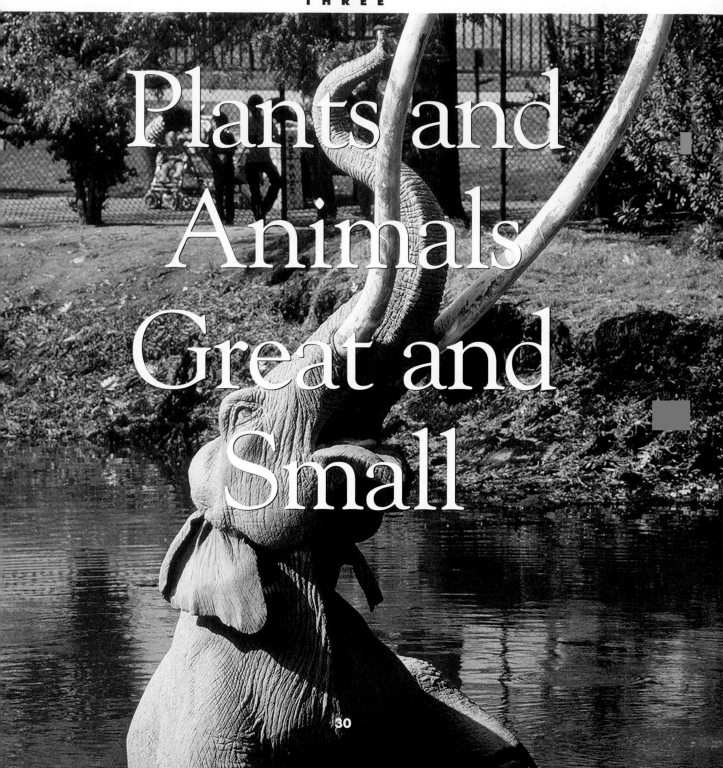

Plants and Animals Great and Small

A DEEP ROAR TINGED WITH FRIGHT ECHOES ACROSS the valley. A saber-toothed tiger is sinking into a pool of black, gummy tar that surrounds a bubbling spring. The thirsty animal had gone to get freshwater, but has become stuck in the goo. The more the tiger struggles, the deeper it sinks. The goo eventually swallows the trapped animal.

This incident occurred more than ten thousand years ago in what is now known as the Rancho La Brea Tar Pits in Los Angeles, California. Numerous other prehistoric creatures, from sloths to giant birds, were also captured by the tar. Today, the pits are a famous fossil site. The George C. Page Museum, located at the pits, displays the remains of these almost-forgotten creatures.

Life in the United States was quite different prior to human existence. Rich beds of dinosaur fossils are now found in the Dakotas and in the Southwest. Florida's alligators, as well as sharks in the Gulf of Mexico, are reminders of that era. Woolly mammoths once lived at the edge of retreating glaciers, and massive fish swam in deep lakes. A distant relative of the camel strolled through the Southwest. The skeleton of such a beast is displayed in the New Mexico Museum of Natural History in Albuquerque.

Today there are only a few species of large wild creatures in the United States. Some are herbivores, or plant eaters, while others are carnivores, or meat eaters. Yet others are omnivores, which eat both vegetation and flesh.

Opposite: **The Rancho La Brea Tar Pits in downtown Los Angeles, California, is home to fossil remains of prehistoric animals that became trapped and died in the sticky asphalt bog.**

Plants and Animals Great and Small **31**

American bison are mostly found grazing on the open prairies, in mountainous regions, and in open woodlands.

Native Americans and the Bison

Native Americans used almost everything from the bison. Even the skin from a hind leg made a perfectly fitted moccasin. The skull often had a special place in ceremonies. A white bison was considered sacred, and seeing one brought good luck.

The American Bison

Among the biggest grass eaters today are bison, a more accurate name than buffalo. Compared to true buffalo in Asia and Africa, the American bison has a larger head, humped shoulders, and fourteen pairs of ribs instead of thirteen. An adult male bison can weigh as much as 2,400 pounds (1,100 kilograms). Bison live in herds much like domestic cattle.

Where millions of wild bison once roamed from the East Coast to the Rocky Mountains, barely 500 were alive in 1889. The rest were victims of hunters, who only took the hides and choice pieces of meat. At the turn of the nineteenth century, zoologists began working to save the few remaining bison. Subsequently, their numbers have slowly climbed again. Today several hundred thousand bison graze in havens such as Yellowstone National Park or on licensed privately owned range lands that raise them for food. Some breeders have crossed bison with cattle to raise "beefalo" that provide a lean, protein-rich meat.

Animals in the Wild

Other large animals found in the United States include elk, moose, bighorn sheep, and deer. These creatures are usually hardy and healthy. Carnivores kill and eat sick and injured animals, ensuring that the fittest survive. The largest meat eater in North America is the Kodiak brown bear of Alaska and Canada. One of these male bears can weigh 1,600 pounds (730 kg). Another large bear, the grizzly, has rightfully earned

Moose are the largest and strongest member of the deer family, standing 4 to 6 feet (1 to 9 m) tall and weighing in at 1,800 pounds (820 kg).

its scientific name of *Ursus arctos horribilis*. This bear, which lives in secluded areas of the West, has a fierce disposition and an enormous appetite. A male weighs up to 1,300 pounds (600 kg).

To satisfy a huge appetite this grizzly bear fishes for salmon at a waterfall.

Wolves, members of the dog family, once ranged from Alaska and the Arctic Islands to Mexico.

Like bison, grizzly bears used to be much more plentiful. They could be found throughout the West and as far south as Mexico. Grizzlies have lost most of their habitats to human land use, and they have been heavily hunted. Today, there are fewer than a thousand grizzlies in the lower forty-eight states. Most of the remaining grizzly bears live in Alaska, where efforts are being made to protect them.

Wolves were once found across most of North America. Today wolf packs are found throughout the Upper Midwest. Wolves hunt a variety of animals and contribute to keeping the population of some prey under control. Scientists have a closed society of wolves to study on Isle Royale, a national park 20 miles (32 km) out in Lake Superior. The animals reached the island years ago by running across the frozen lake.

The National Zoo

The 163-acre (66-ha) Smithsonian National Zoological Park in Washington, D.C., was established by Congress in 1889 "for advancement of science and the instruction and recreation of the people." The zoo houses more than 5,500 mammals, birds, reptiles, amphibians, fish, and invertebrates. It was the first zoo established to save animals on the brink of extinction. Today, nearly 130 of the zoo's 480 species of animals are endangered or threatened. The zoo also conducts research and educational programs in biology and other sciences to help conserve the world's wildlife. Many programs are geared toward children.

Once used mainly for its strength and labor, today the horse is used for sports, riding, and racing.

Many domestic animals, such as horses, are not native to the United States. Although their ancestors may have lived here in ancient times, they eventually died out due to changes in climate or other unknown reasons. Horses made a marvelous comeback, however. The various breeds, ranging from muscular Clydesdales to swift Thoroughbreds, now number almost 7 million. The first "modern" horses were imported by Spanish soldiers called *conquistadors* in the 1500s. The nomadic Plains Indians soon began using horses for transport and for war.

The Ponies of Chincoteague

Chincoteague Island, Virginia, is home to the descendants of horses washed ashore centuries ago when a Spanish galleon sank in a storm off the coast. Every July ponies are herded in the Pony Round-Up by the Chincoteague Volunteer Firemen. The ponies then swim from the island to the mainland, where they are auctioned to raise money for the island fire department. The number of ponies that are permitted to graze in the Chincoteague National Wildlife Refuge is 150. Award-winning children's author Marguerite Henry (1902–1997)

based her famous children's book, *Misty of Chincoteague*, on this exciting event.

Big, Brave, But Not Bald—the Eagle

The bald eagle, the national bird of the United States, is a symbol of power and bravery. With its regal look, it is truly the king of birds. The eagle image on the U.S. seal holds arrows in its left claw to embody the country's readiness to protect itself. In its right claw it holds an olive branch, which is the symbol of peace. The bald eagle is not really bald since its head is actually covered with white feathers. This species has been protected by federal law since the 1950s because it almost became extinct.

Since the 1970s, with the banning of certain chemicals and better environmental controls, the bald eagle has made a comeback. Today, there are about 15,000 eagles in the lower forty-eight states. About 35,000 more live in Alaska.

Go, Birds, Go

Hundreds of bird species fly high over the United States. The autumn skies are always peppered with migrating geese and ducks. The wild turkey is a large fowl related to the pheasant and chicken. Benjamin Franklin considered this bird to be the strongest in the wilderness and wanted it to be the national symbol of the United States. After heated discussion, however, the bald eagle got the nod as the country's icon on June 20, 1782. Turkeys remain part of U.S. folklore, particularly in stories about the first Thanksgiving.

The passenger pigeon was not as lucky as the bald eagle. Now extinct, these birds once numbered in the millions and blocked out the sun when they flew. The pigeons settled in nesting areas that measured as much as 30 square miles (78 sq km). The birds began to die out when settlers cut down the

The passenger pigeon was given its name not due to its migrating habits, but because of its search for food in mass numbers.

oak and beech forests in which the birds thrived. In addition, hunters killed tens of thousands of passenger pigeons, which were delicious eating. Since they only produced one egg a season, the birds could not reproduce fast enough and disappeared. The last known passenger pigeon died in 1914. Its body is preserved at the National Museum of Natural History in Washington, D.C.

A Variety of Vegetation

The United States has a broad variety of plants, ranging from ferns to mushrooms to wild roses. With irrigation, plants can be cultivated where the climate or soil ordinarily would not be suitable for them.

The soil of the upper Northeast supports thick stands of pine, while the deep, dark loam of the Midwest is just right for growing soybeans, corn, wheat, and oats. Cactus and sage grow well in the arid ground of the Southwest. The wet bayou

A Southwest desert garden in Arizona is home to a variety of vegetation such as saguaro, palo verde trees, and chainfruit cholla.

Swamps are important natural preserves for fish, birds, and amphibians, which would otherwise become extinct if such areas were destroyed.

country of Louisiana and the swamps of the Southeast are perfect for water-loving cypress and mangrove trees. Dense vegetation and fragrant apple orchards thrive on the northwest coast, which receives a lot of rain. Hawai'i's soil supports a range of plants, from orchids to palm trees.

Protecting Nature's Bounty

In the nineteenth century, acres of towering white pines were cut in the northern states by lumber companies to satisfy the needs of a growing housing and business market. Huge piles of debris were left behind, becoming fuel for forest fires. The Peshtigo fire in far northeastern Wisconsin was one such blaze. On October 8, 1871, the same day as the more famous Great Chicago Fire, more than 1,000 people died when the fire swept over their village. This death toll remains one of the country's worst natural disasters.

In the 1930s, careless farming techniques and drought turned fields in Oklahoma and the lower Midwest into what was called the Dust Bowl. Thousands of families abandoned their dried-out farms and fled elsewhere. Many headed to California, where they hoped would be a garden paradise. Author John Steinbeck wrote his famous novel, *The Grapes of Wrath*, about the plight of these migrants, who were called "Okies." The book became a popular movie.

To prevent a repeat of such a calamity, the U.S. Department of Agriculture carefully oversees farming, timber production, and related issues on behalf of the public. The agencies work hard to strike a favorable balance between society's demands for products and the need for conservation.

Towering Trees

Giant redwoods are among the oldest living plants in the world. They are also the tallest, often reaching 200 to 275 feet (60 to 85 m) high. One tree has even been measured at 368 feet high (112 m). These trees grow along the foggy Pacific Coast from northern California to Oregon, seldom more than 50 miles (80 km) inland. The redwood's thick bark helps it to resist fire. The wood is also resistant to plant diseases and insects, and its durable lumber is highly prized for siding buildings and making decks. The redwood is related to the giant sequoia found in California's Sierra Nevada Mountains. The redwood's scientific name is *Sequoia sempervirens*.

National Refuge System

The U.S. national wildlife refuge system consists of more than 500 sites around the country, totaling 95 million acres (38 million ha). President Theodore Roosevelt launched the program in 1903 to protect Florida's last brown pelican rookery from the demand for feathers for ladies' hats.

The Arctic National Wildlife Refuge (right), one of the system's largest, covers 20 million acres (8 million ha) in northeastern Alaska. It is managed by the U.S. Fish and Wildlife Service of the Interior Department. Caribou, wolves, musk ox, wolverines, snow geese, and other animals are at home here. Coastal lagoons, islands, forests, and mountains provide a variety of habitats for the wildlife to flourish. However, oil and

gas developers hope to tap into the refuge's natural resources. This concerns conservationists who worry that such development will upset the refuge's delicate ecosystem.

The National Flower

The rose is the national flower of United States. It can be grown in all fifty of the United States and has a long history in this country. President George Washington loved roses. A variety he named after his mother is still grown today.

One of the most famous rose gardens is located at the White House in Washington, D.C. The site, off the West Wing, is used for press conferences and receptions and for presenting major proclamations. Several types of gardens have been on the site during various presidential terms. Ellen Wilson, wife of President Woodrow Wilson, was the first to plant a formal rose garden there in 1913. No major changes in her planting occurred until 1962, when Jacqueline Kennedy had the garden redesigned. Other presidential wives have also put their stamp on the Rose Garden. Betty Ford favored yellow roses, Rosalynn Carter loved peach, and Nancy Reagan preferred red.

In 1985, the U.S. Senate passed a resolution naming the rose as the national flower. The U.S. House of Representatives passed a similar resolution in 1986. Also in 1986, President Ronald Reagan signed a proclamation confirming that the rose be the country's national floral emblem.

Step into the Past

The story of the United States is one of struggle, survival, and ultimate triumph. In its early days, simply getting to the New World from Europe was hard work. Imagine traveling aboard a tiny, crowded ship. The food was often bad, and there was little freshwater.

When settlers arrived in the 1600s, there was only wilderness. Trees had to be cleared to create fields. Cows and chickens had to be protected from wild animals. The French moved inland along the St. Lawrence River. The Spanish settled in steamy Florida, the West Coast, and the dry Southwest. The Dutch made their homes in the beautiful Hudson River region. The British settled along the East Coast. European settlers and American Indians generally got along well at first. They traded with each other and were often allies in fighting each other's enemies. This friendship did not last long, however. As more and more Europeans arrived and their villages grew, the American Indians became angry about being pushed off their own land. This led to conflicts affecting the American frontier for the next 200 years.

Settling In

In 1607, a group of hardy businessmen established Jamestown, Virginia, the first permanent British settlement in the New

Opposite: **In American history, the landing of the *Mayflower* in 1620 and the establishment of Plymouth Colony, in the present state of Massachusetts, is a symbol of the daring idealism on which the United States was founded.**

Colonists established the English settlement of Jamestown in 1607. It was the only settlement on the East Coast for thirteen years.

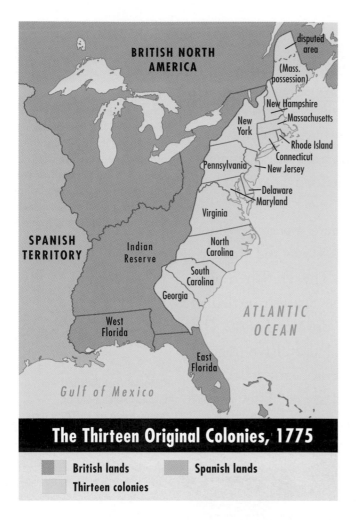

The Thirteen Original Colonies, 1775

British lands

Thirteen colonies

Spanish lands

Map labels: BRITISH NORTH AMERICA, disputed area, (Mass. possession), New Hampshire, Massachusetts, New York, Rhode Island, Connecticut, New Jersey, Pennsylvania, Delaware, Maryland, Virginia, North Carolina, South Carolina, Georgia, Indian Reserve, SPANISH TERRITORY, West Florida, East Florida, Gulf of Mexico, ATLANTIC OCEAN

World. The Pilgrims, religious refugees from England, settled in Plymouth, Massachusetts, in 1620. By that time, the Spanish city of St. Augustine in Florida was over fifty years old, and the French were well established in Canada. Indians had been living in the New Mexican pueblo of Acoma for around a thousand years. This village is considered one of the oldest continuously inhabited communities in North America.

By 1775, there were approximately 2.5 million settlers in the thirteen original British-controlled colonies. The first slaves were imported to Virginia in 1619, and the practice of owning human beings spread throughout the colonies. Most colonists were English, but there were many other Western European nationalities represented, especially Scots, Scots-Irish, and German. British-held Canada was primarily French. The colonies still had a strong economic bond to their various mother countries. Settlers exported flax for the making of linen, as well as codfish, rum, and tobacco.

The colonists were proud of their accomplishments. They did not want to be told what to do by the mother country.

A Historic Community

Bustling Williamsburg was the colonial capital of Virginia. The site was settled in 1633 and incorporated as a city in 1722. Many famous political leaders of early America debated here. General George Washington used the town as his headquarters prior to the battle of Yorktown.

In 1926, philanthropist John D. Rockefeller, Jr., began renovating Williamsburg to preserve its historical character. Dozens of famous buildings were refurbished or reconstructed, and the town became a major tourist site. Guides now act out roles as colonial citizens.

Separated from their original homeland by a century and 3,000 miles of ocean encouraged independent thinking. Britain continued to enforce laws that controlled its colonial trade, however. The king needed money to pay off his war debts, and he depended on the colonies for revenue. The Spanish monarch also used his territories to increase his own coffers.

Opposition to British rule surfaced as early as 1765, following passage of the Stamp Act. This legislation was intended to raise money to pay for the army based in the colonies. The army protected against attacks from other countries and from the American

To strengthen their stronghold, Britain based troops in the growing colonies.

Indians. The British Parliament never asked the colonies if they agreed to the payments. This mistake led to the colonist's rallying cry, "No taxation without representation."

Revolution!

Even though the Stamp Act was never enforced, the stage was set for open revolt. On March 5, 1770, a Boston mob attacked British soldiers, who fired back. Crispus Attucks, a free African American, and three others died in what was called the Boston Massacre. The unrest continued. On December 16, 1773, a group of rebels called the Sons of Liberty disguised themselves as American Indians and dumped tea into Boston Harbor in another tax protest.

A Currier and Ives depiction of the 1773 tax protest known as the Boston Tea Party

The British instituted more restrictive laws. Delegates represented the colonies in the First Continental Congress in 1774. They were called in to deal with these laws. In April 1775, colonial militia attacked British troops who were advancing on Lexington and Concord, Massachusetts, to seize weapons. The revolution had started. On July 4, 1776, the Second Continental Congress adopted the Declaration of Independence.

The long, bloody war ended when the British were finally defeated at Yorktown in 1781. The Treaty of Paris in 1783 solidified the victory. The colonies were granted their

Delegates of Congress in Philadelphia sign the U.S. Declaration of Independence.

independence, and boundaries of the new United States were set. Thousand of colonists who had stayed loyal to Britain during the war, called Tories, fled to Canada, Bermuda, and the Bahamas.

The first U.S. government was organized under the Articles of Confederation, which kept power in the hands of the states rather than in a central, federal government. Leaders such as James Madison and Benjamin Franklin debated about how to improve the system. Their discussions led to the Constitutional Convention of 1787 in Philadelphia, Pennsylvania. After much debate, the Constitution was drawn up. It provided for a strong national government while at the same time allowing the states certain powers. The document went into effect on June 21, 1788. Three years later, an extensive Bill of Rights was added to the Constitution. It established fundamental protection for citizens.

With its hard-won freedom and almost unlimited room to expand, the young United States began to grow. The purchase of Louisiana from France in 1803 doubled

The Louisiana Purchase, 1803

United States   Louisiana Purchase   —— Route of Lewis and Clark

The Lewis and Clark expedition explored vast amounts of uncharted territory of the United States.

the country's size. Scouts and mapmakers such as Meriwether Lewis and William Clark explored the newly acquired territory.

Proving Itself

The young United States still needed to defend itself. The British harassed the new country's shipping and supposedly encouraged American Indians on the frontier to attack

United States Political Families

Two father-son teams have been elected president of the United States. Federalist John Adams was the country's second president, serving from 1797 to 1801, and his son, Democratic-Republican John Quincy Adams, was elected for one term from 1825 to 1829. Republican George H. Bush (far right) was elected in 1989 and served one term. Despite losing the popular vote, his son, George W. Bush (right), was selected as president by a Supreme Court ruling in 2000. The younger Bush's battle with Democratic candidate Al Gore was one of the most fought-over elections in American history.

settlements. Subsequently, the United States declared war on Britain on June 18, 1812. The conflict drew to a close in 1815, although there was no clear winner.

After the war, the U.S. economy prospered as westward expansion continued. More states were added to the Union and there was relative peace during what was called "The Era of Good Feeling." In 1823, President James Monroe issued the Monroe Doctrine. This document warned other nations not to interfere with any country in the Western Hemisphere.

By then, many Americans believed in "Manifest Destiny." They claimed that the United States should control the land between the Atlantic and Pacific Oceans, including the British-held areas in the Northwest and Mexican territories in the Southwest. This attitude contributed to the Mexican War of 1845. Land won by the victorious United States included Texas, the Southwest, and California. The gold rush of 1849 then opened the Far West to thousands of fortune-seekers.

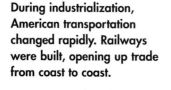

During industrialization, American transportation changed rapidly. Railways were built, opening up trade from coast to coast.

This era also opened the door to the age of industrialization. Raw materials flowed into the country's factories, and finished products poured out. Steamboats, trains, the telegraph, better farming tools such as the cotton gin and the steel plow, advances in health care, and improved education contributed to a sense of well-being. Life was far from wonderful for many, however. This booming economy depended on the labor of millions of slaves.

Political storm clouds gathered, particularly over states' rights and slavery. The Missouri Compromise of 1820 maintained an equal number of slave and free states. When the West opened after the Mexican War, problems developed immediately. Some Americans did not want any restraints against slavery. Abolitionists opposed slavery and helped escaped slaves make their way to freedom via the Underground Railroad. This was a network of hideaways leading toward the Northern states and Canada.

Still other Americans believed in popular sovereignty, saying that citizens in the territories should decide the issue of slavery for themselves. The Kansas-Nebraska Act of 1854 was supposed to resolve this debate by opening the land to legal settlement and by allowing the residents there to determine whether or not they

**Frederick Douglass:
Ardent Abolitionist**

Frederick Douglass (1818–1895) was one of the most important African-American leaders of the nineteenth century. Born in Maryland, he was the son of a slave woman and her white master. He escaped from slavery at age twenty and went on to be a noted writer and speaker. During the Civil War, Douglass advised President Abraham Lincoln on recruiting African-American troops and approaching emancipation issues. He was also a diplomat, representing U.S. interests in Haiti and the Dominican Republic.

Feminist Leader
Elizabeth Cady Stanton

Women's rights advocate Elizabeth Cady Stanton (1815–1902) was born in New York State. She took up women's issues in the 1840s. All through her life, she advocated suffrage, or women's right to vote. This issue was not popular at the time, yet Stanton continued working hard to advance the idea that women were equal to men. While she did not live to see the results of her work, women finally won suffrage with the passage of the 19th Amendment in 1920.

The Union and Confederacy, 1861

Union states   Confederate states   Territories

wanted slavery. Harsh words led to fighting between slavery and anti-slavery forces.

Many people in the South, including those who did not own slaves, felt that their way of life was being threatened. Subsequently, eleven slave states left the Union. They formed a new country called the Confederate States of America. The Union states objected.

War broke out when Confederate troops fired on Fort Sumter on April 12, 1861.

The industrialized Union eventually wore down Confederate resistance. Four years of devastating fighting resulted in 600,000 dead, with social repercussions that still exist today. In some pockets of the South, the Civil War is referred to as the War of Northern Aggression.

Legislation after the war, during the period known as Reconstruction, was intended to improve the lot of freed slaves. Not everyone agreed with these laws. Radical groups such as the Ku Klux Klan sought to deny African Americans their rights, often with violent action such as lynching.

Located on an island in the harbor of Charleston, South Carolina, Fort Sumter was the target of a bombardment that began the Civil War in 1861.

Defender of His People

The great Sioux chief Sitting Bull (1834–1890) declared he would never sign a treaty forcing him to live on a reservation. He fought at the Battle of Little Bighorn, in which Lieutenant Colonel George Custer and all his men were killed. After the Sioux victory, Sitting Bull fled to Canada, but he eventually returned to surrender in 1881. In 1885, he toured with the Buffalo Bill Wild West Show.

Sitting Bull made no effort to halt the Ghost Dance, a spiritual movement that believed that someday all the whites would disappear and the bison would return. The U.S. government sent tribal police to arrest him. In a fight outside his cabin on December 15, 1890, Sitting Bull was killed.

Economic Boom Time

Italian laborers contributed to the 1900 railway construction in upstate New York.

The United States experienced a boom after the Civil War. Railroads united the country. People moved to cities for jobs. The middle class expanded. Handy devices such as the typewriter, the automobile, and the electric light were invented. Between 1870 and 1916, more than 25 million new immigrants found their way to the United States from all over the world. This huge labor pool, plus the country's rich supply of resources, fueled economic growth.

The victory of the United States in the Spanish-American War of 1898 demonstrated the nation's military might. However, the country remained reluctant to be involved in international affairs, even when it entered World War I on the side of its European allies in 1917. With victory and declaration of peace in 1918, the U.S. Senate still rejected American participation in the League of Nations. It was hoped that the league, an organization of many countries around the world, would help preserve peace. America, however, was not interested in joining.

The country continued to be wrapped up in its own affairs throughout the 1920s. A law called Prohibition outlawed the sale of alcohol. While reformers praised the legislation, it actually caused more problems than it resolved. Many ignored the law, and the amendment was finally repealed. During this

Between 1920 and 1930 the United States enforced a law to prohibit people from drinking alcohol. This 1921 photo shows officials seizing barrels of wine In New York.

period, most Americans invested heavily in the stock market. This led to speculation, where investors bought on credit. Eventually, the entire market system collapsed in 1929.

World War II Breaks Out

The Great Depression, a worldwide economic catastrophe, lasted throughout the 1930s. Banks closed, farmers lost their land, and millions were out of work. These difficult times continued until the United States entered World War II in 1941. The war had already been raging in Asia and in Europe by the time the Americans joined the fight. Quickly, the country's industrial might was put to work producing tanks, planes, and guns. More than 15 million men and women joined the military.

Men and women contributed to the war effort in 1942 by working together to build B-24 bombers and transport planes.

The war in Europe ended on May 7, 1945. Japan surrendered the following September, after the United States dropped two atomic bombs on Hiroshima and Nagasaki. The United States became the undisputed leader of the Western world after World War II. There was still tension, however, even with the establishment of the United Nations, another international organization committed to resolve issues without fighting. The Communist Bloc of Eastern European nations, led by the Soviet Union and China, faced off with the United States and its allies in what became known as the cold war. From 1950 to 1953, the United States and other United Nations forces were involved in a bloody conflict in Korea. Non-communist South Korea fought against communist North Korea and its Chinese allies.

The U.S. postwar business sector continued to expand. Television outpaced the movies as a popular form of entertainment. Affluent families moved to the suburbs. At the same time, poorer people were left behind in crumbling municipalities. In some areas of the country, particularly in the South, public places were still segregated by race. Courageous activists of all races protested these inequities with boycotts, marches, and voter registration drives. When African-American leader Dr. Martin Luther King Jr. was assassinated in 1968, riots burned out the core of more than a dozen cities.

Turmoil Continues

The Vietnam War brought additional turmoil. There were draft protests, widespread drug use, and scandals during the years of President Richard Nixon's administration. Eventually the war ended, Nixon left office, and the country persevered through a cycle of economic challenges and additional unrest overseas. The animosity of the cold war decreased as the collapse of the Soviet Union in 1991 led to better relationships between the new Russia and the United States. In 1991, during the Persian Gulf War, the United States led a coalition of allies against Iraq after that Middle Eastern nation invaded its neighbor, oil-rich Kuwait.

Ten years later came the horror of September 11, 2001, when terrorists crashed commercial planes into the World

On September 11, 2001, two hijacked planes crashed into and destroyed New York's World Trade Center in one of the most horrific displays of world terrorism.

Trade Center in New York City and the Pentagon in Washington, D.C. Thousands of people were killed. Suddenly, the United States did not seem as safe as before. To deal with the challenge, the government increased security at airports, power plants, and similar potential targets.

Forces led by U.S. troops swept into remote Afghanistan in pursuit of leaders who plotted the attack. Led by Saudi exile Osama bin Laden, the radical Islamist group al-Qaeda took credit for the attacks. The group was based in Afghanistan and supported by the Taliban government there. On October 7, 2001, allied forces entered Afghanistan and began to drive the Taliban from power. Many al-Qaeda and Taliban fighters were killed or captured. However, Osama bin Laden was not apprehended and continued to send messages urging other extremists to carry on the fight.

The United States again turned its attention to Iraq, claiming that this Middle Eastern country had hidden weapons of mass destruction and was harboring al-Qaeda operatives. Presenting its case before the United Nations in 2003, the United States pushed for a war to drive Iraqi president Saddam Hussein from power. On March 19, 2003, U.S. and coalition forces began dropping bombs over Iraq.

The terrorist attack of September 11 did not bring about the collapse of the United States—far from it. The turmoil only encouraged a stronger sense of civic unity. As images from that awful day slid deeper into the nation's collective memory, the country again slowly turned toward its future.

Let Freedom Ring

Even after the American Revolution, the founders of the United States favored the British system of representatives working on behalf of the people, who are guaranteed basic civil rights. However, an American spirit of independence and individual responsibility was further nurtured and strengthened by life on the frontier.

The United States of America is a republic, where the ultimate power rests with the voters who select their representatives. The national government is based on laws contained in the Constitution and its amendments. There are three branches of government: executive, legislative, and judicial.

The president (executive) enforces laws passed by Congress (legislative), and the Supreme Court (judicial) interprets the laws whenever questions arise. The three branches also have powers that overlap each other. For example, the president can veto legislation by Congress, but Congress also has the power to pass bills over a veto. This system, called checks and balances, keeps any one branch of government from becoming too powerful.

The federal government makes laws, collects taxes, enforces security, coins money, builds highways, and performs other services. It shares other powers with the fifty states. The states have certain rights guaranteed them by the Constitution, including enforcing local laws and taxation. The federal government cannot get rid of states or redraw their boundaries.

Opposite: **The Lincoln Memorial in Washington, D.C., commemorates the sixteenth president of the United States and his dedication to preserve the Union and abolish slavery.**

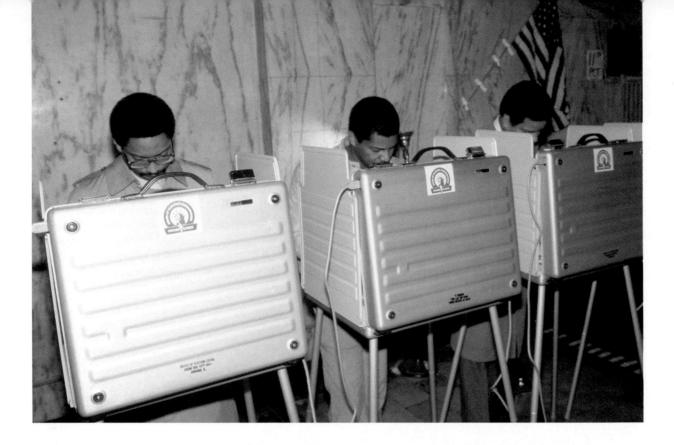

At the age of 18, all U.S. citizens have the right to vote for their leaders.

In the United States, citizens have the right to elect their national, state, and local leaders. They are also able to vote on certain issues. It is the responsibility of the electorate to be informed about all sides of a question and to know about candidates so they can make wise decisions. A good citizen stays involved in the electoral process. Attending forums, staying up-to-date on current affairs, and handing out campaign materials are among the many ways a citizen can participate in the political process.

The Executive Branch

The executive branch consists of the president's office, the executive departments, and several independent agencies.

The president is the head of the government and the chief of state. He or she lives and works in the White House, an impressive building located in Washington, D.C. The president is responsible for making sure federal laws are enforced. He also appoints, with Senate consent, certain federal officials such as judges. The president is commander in chief of the military and represents the United States when dealing with other nations. He or she also performs many ceremonial duties. According to the Constitution, the president can only serve two four-year terms. He or she must be 35 years of age or older. The office must be held by a natural-born citizen who has lived in the United States at least fourteen years.

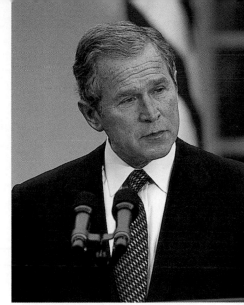

George W. Bush, president of the United States

The United States Flag

No one is sure who designed the first American flag. Some historians say that New Jersey congressman Francis Hopkinson made the original image, while others believe it was Betsy Ross, a Philadelphia seamstress.

Regardless of who made the first flag, the Continental Congress passed the first Flag Act on June 14, 1777. It read: "Resolved, that the flag of the United States be thirteen stripes, alternate red and white; that the union be thirteen stars, white in a blue field, representing a new constellation."

Over the years, various laws governed the flag's design. An executive order by President Eisenhower, dated August 21, 1959, provided for the arrangement of the stars in nine rows staggered horizontally and eleven columns staggered vertically.

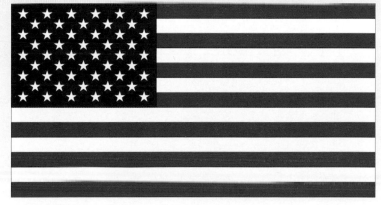

The Electoral College

In the United States, voters do not directly elect the president and vice president. This is done through the Electoral College, which is not a real school but individuals chosen by party leaders in every state. Each state has as many electoral votes as the total of its senators and representatives in Congress. In the December following a presidential election, the electors of every state and the District of Colombia gather to vote. They usually cast their ballots for the candidate supported by their respective political party.

The electors' votes are sealed and sent to the president of the Senate and the administrator of General Services in Washington, D.C. The ballots are opened in January at a joint session of Congress. One Republican and one Democrat from each house count the votes.

The candidate who gets the majority of electoral votes is named winner.

Over the years, there have been many proposals to abolish the Electoral College and to allow the people to vote directly for both president and vice president. Opponents have rightly said that under the Electoral College system, candidates can win even if they receive a minority of popular votes.

In the 2000 election, Republican George W. Bush was selected president by a five-to-four decision of the United States Supreme Court. A close popular vote and confusion over a recount in Florida took the case to the country's highest court, which ruled in favor of Bush over Al Gore, the Democratic candidate. This may support the demand to change the system for future presidential elections.

The executive office also includes several other divisions, including that of the vice president, the Office of Management and Budget, and the National Security Council.

Fourteen executive departments administer the national government: State, Treasury, Defense, Justice, Interior, Agriculture, Commerce, Labor, Health and Human Services, Housing and Urban Development,

President George W. Bush and members of his cabinet

Transportation, Energy, Education, and Veteran's Affairs. The heads of thirteen departments are called secretaries, while the director of the Justice Department is the Attorney General. They are all appointed by the president and approved by the Senate. These men and women form the president's cabinet.

In 2001, after the September 11 terrorist attack on the United States, President Bush set up the Office of Homeland Security. In 2002, this became a new cabinet department. Under Bush, cabinet-level rank also has been accorded to the administrator of the Environmental Protection Agency, the director of the Office of Management and Budget, the director of National Drug Control Policy, and the United States Trade Representative.

NATIONAL GOVERNMENT OF THE UNITED STATES

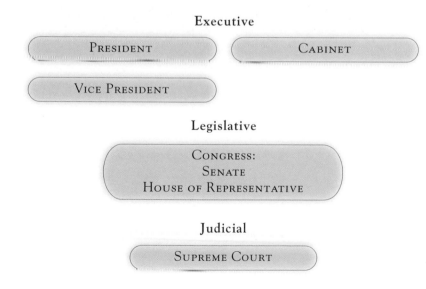

Executive

PRESIDENT   CABINET

VICE PRESIDENT

Legislative

CONGRESS:
SENATE
HOUSE OF REPRESENTATIVE

Judicial

SUPREME COURT

The National Anthem

During the War of 1812, young attorney Francis Scott Key was aboard a British warship in the harbor of Baltimore, Maryland. He was trying to free an American friend who was a prisoner. On September 13, 1814, the British attacked Fort McHenry, an American fortress guarding the city. The fort withstood the fierce bombardment. Key was so impressed that he wrote a four-stanza poem about it. The verses were soon set to music. Congress made the poem the national anthem on March 3, 1931.

A copy of Key's poem is displayed in the Library of Congress. The flag that inspired him can be seen at the Smithsonian Institution's National Museum of American History in Washington, D.C.

"The Star-Spangled Banner"
(first and last stanzas)

Oh say, can you see, by the dawn's early light,
What so proudly we hail'd at the twilight's last gleaming?
Whose broad stripes and and bright stars, thro' the perilous fight,
O'er the ramparts we watch'd, were so gallantly streaming?
And the rockets' red glare, the bombs bursting in air,
Gave proof thro' the night that our flag was still there.
Oh say, does that star-spangled banner yet wave
O'er the land of the free and the home of the brave?

Oh thus be it ever when freemen shall stand
Between their lov'd home and the war's desolation,
Blest with vict'ry and peace, may the heav'n-rescued land
Praise the Pow'r that hath made and preserved us a nation!
Then conquer we must, when our cause it is just,
And this be our motto: "In God is our trust!"
And the star-spangled banner in triumph shall wave
O'er the land of the free and the home of the brave!

The Legislative Branch

The legislative branch of government is Congress, which is made up of the Senate and the House of Representatives. There are also eight administrative agencies in this branch, ranging from the Architect of the Capitol to the United States Botanic Garden.

The Senate has one hundred members, or two from each state, who serve six-year terms. The vice president presides over the Senate and votes only in case of a tie. The Senate approves treaties and authorizes the president's choices for major federal positions.

There are more than 400 members in the House of Representatives, each serving two-year terms. Every state has at least one member, and the rest of its representatives are based on population. This figure is determined every ten years in a process called reapportionment. The Speaker, a member of the majority party, presides over House sessions.

At a State of the Union Address, the president delivers a speech to both the Senate and the House of Representatives.

Powerful committees do much of Congress's work. They examine all proposed legislation. The committees then can recommend, turn down, or table (set aside) the bills. In addition to separate committees, there are a few joint committees that discuss atomic energy, taxation, immigration policy, and other important issues.

A bill can be introduced either in the House or the Senate. If the House passes a bill, it goes to the Senate, which turns it over to the appropriate committee for study. After considering the bill, the committee can okay a bill and present it to the full Senate, which then votes. Sometimes amendments are added to the bill. Only the House can introduce a revenue bill.

If the two chambers have difficulty in agreeing on legislation, they can set up a joint committee to work out a compromise. When the bill is finally approved, it is sent to the president, who can either sign it into law or veto it. Congress has the power to override, or cancel, the president's vote.

The Supreme Court is the country's top judicial body, with members appointed for life. They are an integral part of the country's governmental system of checks and balances.

The Judicial Branch

The Supreme Court consists of a chief justice and eight associate justices. They are all appointed for life by the president and approved by the Senate. There are about ninety federal district courts located around the country, along with thirteen federal courts of appeals. All these judges are also appointed for life by the president, with the Senate's approval. A decision made in a district court regarding federal laws can be appealed, or challenged, to an appeals court. It can also be sent on to the Supreme Court for a final ruling.

Political Parties

Among the colony's earliest political parties were the Whigs, who supported the American Revolution. The Tories supported the king of England. After the war, many other political groups sprang up. Among them were the National Republicans, the Anti-Masonic Party, the Constitutional Union Party, and the Democratic-Republican Party.

The young country's main political parties were the Federalists and the Democratic-Republicans. The Federalists soon died out, as did others such as the Whigs and the Anti-Masonic Party. The Democratic-Republican Party continued and, in the late 1820s, renamed itself the Democratic Party. This is the party we know today.

The Republicans, or Grand Old Party (GOP), date back to 1854, when anti-slavery advocates gathered in Ripon, Wisconsin. By the time of the Civil War, the Republicans and the Democrats had become the two major political organizations.

Over the ensuing generations, the Republican Party evolved into a group primarily advocating conservative and business-related causes. The Republican symbol is that of the elephant. The Democrats also underwent many changes.

The elephant, symbol of the Republican party

Two inflatable donkeys identify delegates at a Democratic national convention.

Many southern Democrats were among those favoring secession (withdrawal from the union) prior to the Civil War. The party eventually grew into one generally considered liberal and labor-oriented. The donkey is the Democratic symbol. The United States continues to have a two-party system, although a number of minority parties bring spirited debate to the national scene.

The Role of the States

The state governments maintain law and order, regulate business, and oversee education. The state has authority over local governments that run cities, towns, villages, and school districts. Each of the fifty states has its own constitution, plus a bill of rights.

A popularly elected governor is in charge of each state's executive branch. He or she can appoint officials, direct the state militia, and sign or veto bills. In most states, voters elect officers in the executive branch, including a lieutenant governor, secretary of state, treasurer, auditor, and attorney general. However, in some cases the governor or legislature names one or the other of these officials.

Every state but Nebraska has two houses in its legislative branch, which is usually called a general or legislative assembly. Senators serve four-year terms, while those in the lower house serve either two- or four-year terms. Most assemblies meet annually to conduct business, but a few gather only every two years. If the governor wishes, a special assembly can be called to deal with emergencies. Most of the assembly's work occurs in committees.

The judicial branch of a state's government handles both criminal and civil offenses. A supreme court heads this branch. While most judges are elected, the governors in several states appoint the members of the high court.

While the states have a lot of authority, the Constitution limits their power. A single state cannot negotiate a treaty with another country; nor can it regulate interstate commerce. A state cannot issue its own money.

Most of the states are divided into smaller units of government called counties, a word derived from a French term meaning "land belonging to a count." In Louisiana, these are called parishes. The power, form, and size of county government depend on the individual states. The counties can be managed by an elected executive, backed by a county board. A county is responsible for maintaining roads, administering jails, and aiding the poor and sick. It also manages parks, hospitals, zoos, airports, and libraries, and ensures water purification and garbage pickup.

Municipal, or city, governments are responsible for local police departments, urban renewal, and the arts. City government can consist of a mayor and city council or a council-manager format. Under the first, the mayor acts independently of the council. Under the second, a professional city manager is hired by the city council and carries out its directives, as well as managing all its services.

Washington, D.C.: Did You Know This?

Washington is the capital of the United States and is the only city not part of a state. It also is the seat of the federal government. The city, which covers the entire District of Columbia, is located on the east side of the Potomac River. The District of Columbia comprises land managed by the federal government.

The cornerstone of the Capitol building, which houses Congress, was laid on September 18, 1793. The president's home, the White House, was completed in 1798 and other buildings sprang up around it to house the Treasury and other government departments. During the War of 1812, the British captured Washington and burned most of the public buildings on August 24, 1814. During the Civil War, Washington was threatened several times by approaching Confederate forces. Its defenses were never attacked.

The local government of Washington is a combination of city and federal responsibilities. Two-thirds of the city revenue comes from taxes, while the rest comes from the federal government.

Today, 572,059 people live in the District of Columbia. More than 40,000 residents are citizens of other countries who work in embassies or for international organizations.

Many of the nation's most familiar landmarks are in Washington, D.C.: the towering

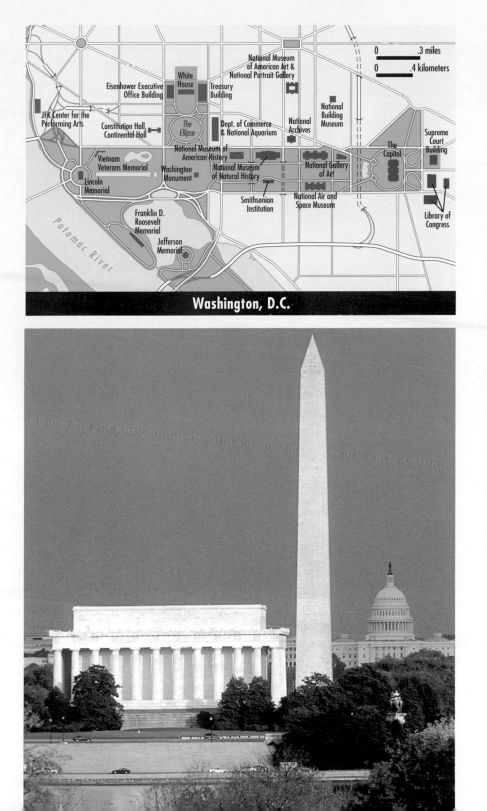

Washington, D.C.

Washington Monument, the imposing Capitol, the Vietnam Veterans Memorial, the Lincoln Memorial, and the John F. Kennedy Center for the Performing Arts are among them. The Smithsonian Institution acts as the "nation's attic" by collecting and displaying historical artifacts.

During the summer the weather is often hot and muggy. The temperature in July ranges between 71° to 89°F (22° to 31°C). Winter is usually mild, although it can be cold and rainy. Snow brings the city to a standstill, as it did in a massive storm in February 2003. Without proper cleanup equipment, the job of snow removal is very difficult. The average temperature in January is 27° to 42°F (−3° to 6°C).

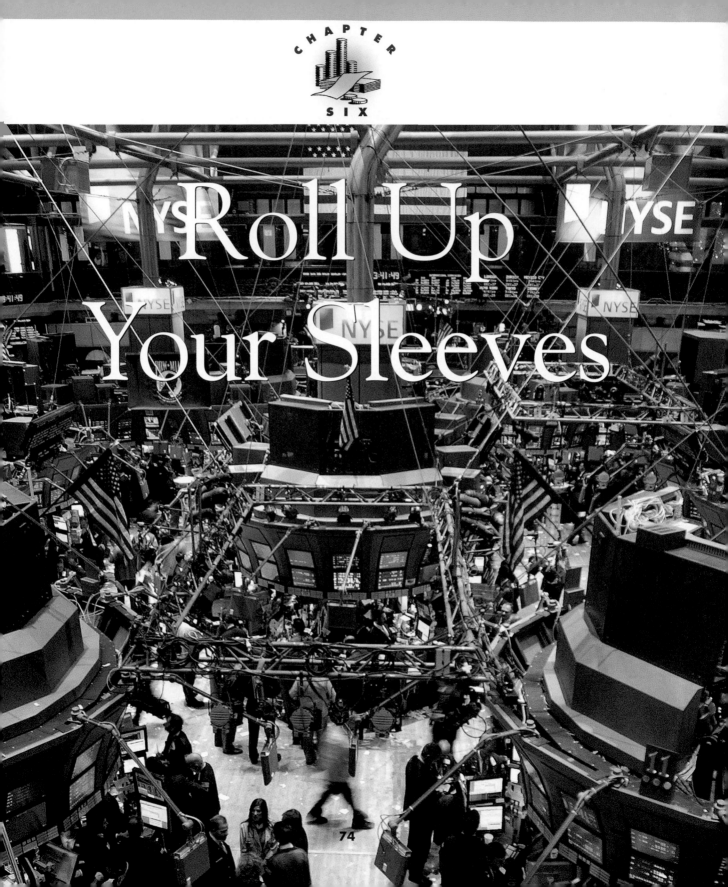

Roll Up Your Sleeves

The United States economy is one of the strongest in the world. There are many reasons for this success. Among them, the country has an abundance of natural resources, including fresh water. There are vast deposits of minerals such as coal, copper, lead, and zinc, as well as excellent soil for growing crops.

Factors such as an educated workforce, private money for investment, an abundance of research, and talented managers making informed decisions have long fueled the United States' business machine.

One of the first manufacturing plants in the United States was a tiny glass-making kiln in colonial Jamestown, Virginia. The nation's expansive network of mills and factories evolved from that humble beginning. In addition to manufacturing, the country has a strong service industry. Industries such as insurance, tourism, hospitality, finance, transportation, and medical provide help to consumers.

Companies do not have to be as large as General Motors, IBM, or Dow Chemical in order to contribute to the economy. Small businesses that employ only a few workers do their

Opposite: **Stock traders work on the busy New York Stock Exchange floor buying and selling orders of stocks according to the laws of supply and demand.**

Weights and Measures

The United States uses the common system of measurement, unlike most of the rest of the world, which uses the metric system. The basic units of weight are the ounce, pound, and ton. The basic measurements of distance are the inch, foot, yard, and mile. Liquids are measured in pints, quarts, and gallons. Even cooking has its own method of measuring, including teaspoons, tablespoons, and cups. Temperatures are indicated by Fahrenheit degrees, while the metric system uses Celsius measurements.

share. Some people prefer to work for themselves. Even kids mowing lawns contribute to the economy. In exchange for this service, they earn money to pay for new CDs, movie tickets, or clothing purchases at the mall.

The U.S. economy is tied to that of the rest of the world. American companies need to sell their products and services internationally to be profitable. Firms sometimes move their assembly plants to countries where labor is cheaper, taxes are lower, and environmental or safety regulations are not as strong as in the United States. These business owners say that the move is necessary to keep production costs low. When a company moves elsewhere, however, it often places a lot of American employees out of work.

What the United States Grows, Makes, and Mines

Agriculture

Cattle and calves	105 million head
Milk production	12.2 billion pounds
Corn	8.5 billion bushels

Manufacturing

Chemicals	$191 billion
Electronics	$181 billion
Industrial machinery	$167.6 billion

Mining

Coal	1.07 billion short tons (973.9 million metric tons)
Iron ore	61,000,000 metric tons
Copper	1,450,000 metric tons
Gold	353 metric tons

Capitalism at Work

The United States has a capitalist economy. It is controlled by individuals and businesses rather than by the government. Under capitalism, companies decide what to make. The market—current measurements of supply and demand—determines how much of any item will be produced and how much it will cost. Investors buy stock in firms. This provides money for the company to purchase new equipment or to expand its operations. When a company does well and earns profits, investors get back their money and earn more.

Bally's Casino in Las Vegas, Nevada designs and manufactures its own electronic games of chance.

This system usually works well. Sometimes companies are not managed well, and they collapse. This contributed to the downfall of the Enron Corporation in 2001, followed by WorldCom in 2002. These are two of the largest business failures in U.S. history.

Sometimes, the market just does not work out for some businesses, or they peak too soon. As an example, the dot-com technology industry was supposed to bring on a new wave of prosperity in the 2000s. Instead, dozens of high-rolling technology firms failed. Often, their systems were not in place to provide a final quality product. Many start-up companies could not even offer support to their customers.

Making Microsoft Go

William H. (Bill) Gates, chairman of Microsoft Corporation, was born October 28, 1955. He and his two sisters grew up in Seattle. Their father is a lawyer, and their late mother was a schoolteacher. Gates became interested in computers while he was in grade school; he was already writing programs when he was thirteen years old.

Gates dropped out of Harvard University to turn all his energies to Microsoft, a company he started in 1975. He and his partners believed that the personal computer would be a valuable aid both for office and home use.

Gates's vision paid off, and the company prospered. Under his leadership, Microsoft invested billions of dollars in research and development of products.

Gates also donated more than $4.5 billion to public health, civic, and arts charities.

Money Facts

Both coins and paper money are used in the United States. Only the federal government has the authority to produce money. In 1792, Congress established the dollar as the basic unit of currency.

Several American presidents are featured on U.S. currency. President Abraham Lincoln is on the penny, the 1-cent coin. President Thomas Jefferson is featured on the nickel, a coin valued at 5 cents. President Franklin D. Roosevelt is on the dime (10 cents). The quarter (25 cents) features President George Washington. President John F. Kennedy and the presidential seal are on the half dollar (50 cents). There are two $1 coins. One features women's rights leader Susan B. Anthony, and the other has American Indian guide Sacagawea.

President George Washington and the Great Seal of the United States grace the $1 bill. President Thomas Jefferson and the signing of the Declaration of Independence are the graphics on the $2 bill. On the $5 bill, look for Lincoln again. Founding Father Alexander Hamilton peers out from the $10 bill. President Andrew Jackson is featured on the $20 bill, with President Ulysses S. Grant on the $50 bill. Benjamin Franklin is featured on the $100 bill.

Manufacturing Muscle

Manufacturing is the most important piece of the economic pie in the United States. It accounts for about 20 percent of the gross domestic product (GDP). The GDP measures the monetary value of all goods and services produced in a country in any given year. Factories turn out durable goods, such as garden hoses and auto tires. They also make producer goods, such as sheet steel, which can be transformed into many other products. In the 1960s and 1970s, numerous factories in the North and Northeast closed due to competition from overseas or other market factors. For a while, this part of the country was called the Rust Belt because of all the abandoned plants. An oil exploration boom in the South also went bust around the same time.

Manufacturing drives the U.S. economy. Automobile manufacturing generates almost 4 percent of the nation's output and provides jobs for millions of workers.

By the 2000s, however, most of the hardest-hit communities had made a turnaround. Service industries such as insurance firms replaced many factory jobs. Indianapolis, for instance, decided to capitalize on the sports industry. It is now home to numerous athletic association headquarters. Often, depressed areas emphasize tourism to attract fresh outside money.

Despite these economic challenges, the U.S. manufacturing sector remains powerful. When one area slumps, another does well. Ports remain busy. They ship chemicals, food products, industrial machinery, and thousands of other products around the world. In return, coffee beans, cocoa, automobiles, and clothing are imported to the United States.

Shipping containers are piled high atop a cargo ship in a U.S. port.

LUDWIGSHAFEN EXPRESS
HAMBURG

Agreements with other nations help to maintain a favorable balance of trade for the United States. One such partnership, the North American Free Trade Agreement (NAFTA), links Canada, the United States, and Mexico. NAFTA allows goods to flow freely from one country to the other.

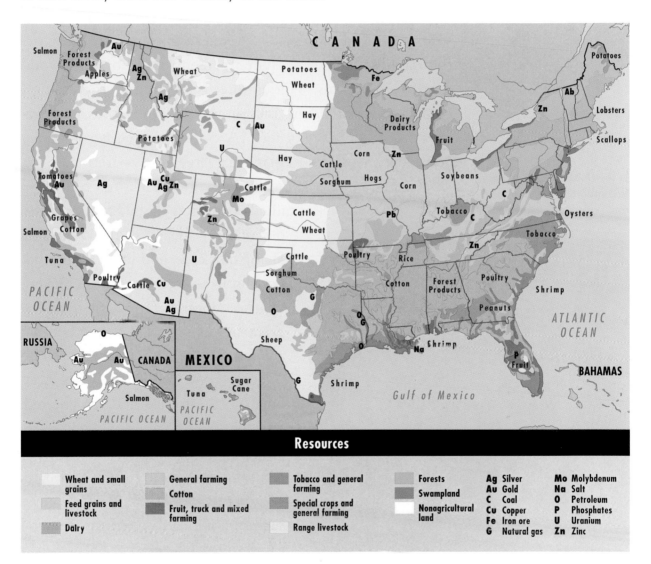

Resources

Wheat and small grains	General farming	Tobacco and general farming	Forests	**Ag** Silver **Mo** Molybdenum
Feed grains and livestock	Cotton	Special crops and general farming	Swampland	**Au** Gold **Na** Salt
Dairy	Fruit, truck and mixed farming	Range livestock	Nonagricultural land	**C** Coal **O** Petroleum
				Cu Copper **P** Phosphates
				Fe Iron ore **U** Uranium
				G Natural gas **Zn** Zinc

At the time of the Revolutionary War, most American people worked on farms. The invention of the steel plow and the planter improved cultivation, and the breeding of healthy livestock made rural life a lot easier. On the other hand, not as many agricultural workers were needed. This caused a huge shift in society as thousands of Americans moved to the cities to find jobs. Today, less than 3 percent of the nation's workforce is on farms. Agriculture is becoming increasingly computerized. Programs track animal growth records and measure proper amounts of feed. A college degree is sometimes considered necessary to manage a large farm operation.

In the United States, chicken is consumed more than beef and pork.

Raising animals is big business in the United States. In 2000, the government tallied 60 million pigs; 97 million cows; 6.7 million sheep; and 335 million laying chickens, and more than 8 billion broilers used as eating chickens on the country's farms and ranches. Some animals are not penned up but are free-range. Others are raised in "factory farms" where they are confined until fattened and slaughtered. Residents of agricultural states are concerned about the smell and waste runoff from these large facilities. Meanwhile, suppliers say they need such operations to meet the demand for fresh food.

The U.S. Department of Agriculture ensures that there are sales outlets for farm produce and provides reports on production. It also researches plant and animal diseases. States also have departments of agriculture to help their own farmers care for and sell their products. Some parts of the country are noted for certain food products. Maine lobsters, Idaho potatoes, Michigan cherries, Washington apples, Wisconsin cheese, Florida oranges, Texas beef, Kansas wheat, and Iowa corn are sold all over the world.

Looking After U.S. Workers

The U.S. Department of Labor is responsible for seeing that laws protecting workers are enforced. It also oversees federal funds used to train those out of work. Labor Day, which honors workers, is a legal holiday. The day is celebrated with picnics, parades, and speeches on the first Monday of

The U.S. workforce is made up of more than 140 million men and women, working in a variety of occupations from laborers to executives.

September. In 2002, there were 142 million people employed in the United States and 8.6 million unemployed people. Some corporate executives make millions of dollars a year, plus benefits that range from health-insurance plans to country-club memberships. According to the law, workers are entitled to a minimum wage of $5.15 an hour. Most Americans work until retirement, when they are 65 years old. Many active older people now stay at their jobs longer or launch another career when they reach that age.

About 65 million women are in the workforce. Some are laborers, while others are highly paid executives. The need for extra workers during World War II opened the door to women entering the labor pool. Women are still fighting to be paid the same wages as men.

Unions were organized in the United States to improve conditions and secure better wages for workers. Early in the industrial age, laborers had little or no protection. They worked long hours in unsafe conditions for little pay. Imagine trying to feed a family on only a few dollars a day. During the nineteenth century, children aged seven to twelve worked in dangerous factories and coal mines. Today, some children travel with their families from farm to farm to pick fruit and vegetables. These are itinerant, or migrant, workers, many of whom are in the United States illegally.

Unions negotiate with employers on behalf of the workers. Occasionally, employees and managers cannot work out a contract, and the workers strike. Companies might hire "scabs," a name for workers who replace the striking union members. Labor disputes can turn violent. One of the worst was the Homestead Strike of 1892, in which steelworkers walked out at the giant Carnegie Steel Company. Private guards hired by the company killed several strikers.

The first unions in the United States were formed in the 1800s. The

Striking workers encourage passersby to support their union and strike.

Knights of Labor and the National Labor Union of the 1860s were followed by the American Federation of Labor, the Congress of Industrial Organizations, the Industrial Workers of the World, and others. Among the great labor leaders in the United States were Samuel Gompers, president of the American Federation of Labor; Walter Reuther, president of the United Auto Workers; and Cesar E. Chavez, who founded the United Farm Workers.

Over the years, concerned legislators pushed laws to help workers. President Franklin D. Roosevelt signed the National Industrial Recovery Act of 1933. This law guaranteed a minimum wage, allowed union bargaining, and said that workers had the right to join unions. Today, labor organizations are challenged by automation, in which machines replace workers. There is also a decline in the number of workers who join unions.

A Nation of Immigrants

I MAGINE LEAVING YOUR HOMELAND TO MAKE A FRESH START in the United States. Maybe relatives sent letters telling what it would be like. You are very excited but a little frightened, too. A century ago, you would have arrived by sea. You rush to find a place by the railing of your passenger ship and stare over the water. There it is, New York Harbor and the Statue of Liberty! It is the most beautiful sight you have ever seen.

Today, you may arrive by airplane. Or perhaps you sneak into the country because your family desperately wants to find work in the United States, or they are fleeing oppression in their country. Regardless of how you arrived, you now are in the United States of America, where you believe anything is possible.

Opposite: **Photographed by Lewis Hine, an Italian mother and her children arrive at Ellis Island in 1905.**

Lady Liberty

The Statue of Liberty is located in New York Harbor on Liberty Island. The statue was a gift from the people of France to the United States. She was dedicated by President Grover Cleveland on October 28, 1886. The statue has become a worldwide symbol of political freedom and opportunity. The tablet in her hand reads "July 4, 1776" in Roman numerals.

The statue is dressed in a flowing gown like an ancient Roman goddess and wears a spiked crown on her head. She stands 151 feet, 1 inch (46.05 m) from the base to her torch. Her index finger is 8 feet (2.44 m) long, and her mouth is three feet (1 m) wide. There are 354 steps to reach her crown. The copper in the statue weighs 31 tons (34 metric tons) and the weight of her steel is 125 tons (138 metric tons). The concrete foundation weighs 27,000 tons (30 metric tons).

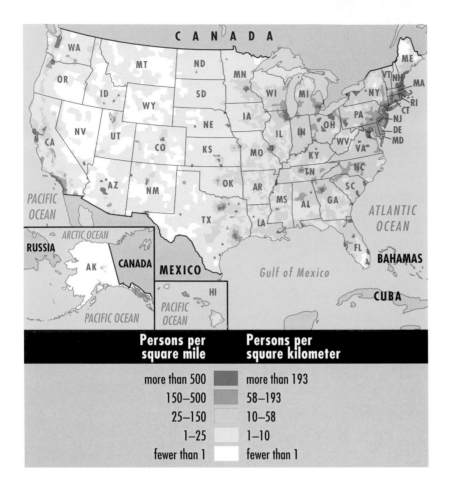

Persons per square mile

more than 500	
150–500	
25–150	
1–25	
fewer than 1	

Persons per square kilometer

more than 193	
58–193	
10–58	
1–10	
fewer than 1	

A flood of people came to the United States over the centuries. But how many people now live here? The Constitution mandates that a census be taken every ten years, in the years ending in "0." A census is important because it determines how many seats an individual state may have in the U.S. House of Representatives. The figures are also used to establish congressional boundaries, to allocate federal and state funds, and to help with policy decisions. The nation's first census was taken in 1790. It recorded about 4 million people. Of this total, 3.2 million were of European origin, and almost 760,000 were African Americans, most of whom were slaves.

Who Are We?

The 2000 census counted 281,421,906 persons living in the United States. Of that number, 225,981,679 live in urban areas. Only 59,063,597 live in the country, with 4,800,000 on farms. California is the most populous state, with 33,871,648

Population of the Largest U.S. Cities (2000 est.)

New York City	8,008,278
Los Angeles	3,694,820
Chicago	2,896,016
Houston	1,953,631
Philadelphia	1,517,550

residents. Wyoming has only 493,782 residents. New York City and its immediate urban area have the most people, numbering 21,199,865.

There are over 200 million people living in the United States comprising of many cultures and ethnic backgrounds.

Language

English is spoken by a majority of U.S. residents, but at least 46 million people speak another language. The most prevalent alternative language is Spanish, followed by various Asian languages. Children with American Indian heritage, as well as others with strong ethnic ties to their ancestral homelands, are learning the languages of their ancestors. This could be anything from Lakota Sioux to Latvian.

The majority of immigrants came to the United States between 1820 and 1975, when 47 million people entered the country. Of that number, 35.9 million came from Europe, 8.3 million arrived from other countries in the Western Hemisphere, and 2.2 million came from Asia. Most of the European arrivals traveled prior to 1924. These nationalities intermarried over the years. Subsequently, there are more and more children with

Common Words and Phrases

Burn the candle at both ends	Work too hard
Bust a gut	Work harder
Get the lead out	Go fast
Go to pot	Become a failure
Fast as greased lightning	Really fast
Hold your horses	Slow down
In the nick of time	Just in time
In the groove	Have a good, fun spirit
Keep under your hat	Keep a secret
Jump the gun	Start too soon
Like a bull in a china shop	Clumsy
More than one way to skin a cat	More than one way to do something

many ethnic traditions in their family. The 2000 census was the first national count allowing respondents to identify themselves as more than one race.

A Diverse Population

Spectators celebrate the Puerto Rican Day Parade in New York City.

The 35 million Hispanics in the United States are among the most diverse population groups in the country. They include Puerto Ricans, Mexicans, Cubans, Dominicans, and Central and South Americans. About 12 million Asians make up another large group of Americans. Most are of Chinese ancestry, but there

are also Filipino, Pakistani, Asian Indian, Japanese, Korean, Vietnamese, and more than a dozen other nationalities.

In 1924, the country's first Immigration Act established a "national origins quota system," limiting the number of immigrants coming into the United States from some nations, especially from Asia. The Immigration and Nationality Act of 1965 eliminated such restrictions and set up a first-come first-served allocation of visas. A visa is a document allowing an alien, or non-citizen, into the country. Additional overhaul of U.S. immigration laws took place in 1990.

Until an immigrant learns English, the country's primary language, it can

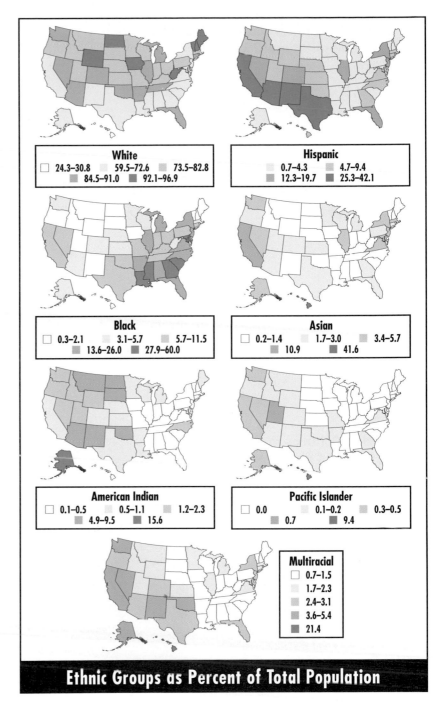

Ethnic Groups as Percent of Total Population

Ethnic Breakdown in National Population (2000 est.)

One race	274,595,678
White	211,460,626
Hispanic or Latino	35,305,818
Black or African American	34,658,190
Asian	10,242,998
American Indian and Alaska Native	2,475,956
Native Hawaiian and other Pacific Islander	398,835
Some other race	5,359,073
Two or more races	6,826,228

be hard to make a home in the United States. In Miami, Los Angeles, Houston, and other cities, Spanish is the major second language due to the large numbers of Hispanics who live there. There are still ethnic urban neighborhoods where grandmothers call out to their grandchildren in Italian or Polish.

When they first arrive, many immigrants have to take low-paying, unskilled jobs. As they integrate into American society, their economic well-being usually improves. Their sons and daughters often do even better. By the third generation, the family is most likely doing quite well. Many immigrant families still celebrate their national traditions, such as Serbian Family Feast Day or the Mexican Day of the Dead.

Native Cultures in the United States

There are more than 2 million American Indians in the United States. The Cherokee Nation is the largest group, followed by the Navajo, Sioux, and Choctaw. They are scattered throughout the country, living on reservations and in big cities. After years of poverty, many Indian nations are using proceeds from tribal gambling casinos to fund projects for their people.

Immigration at Ellis Island

Ellis Island covers about 27 acres (11 ha) in New York Harbor. It has been government property since 1808, when it was an arsenal and a fort. In 1892, it was made into the chief immigration point for new arrivals to this country. Ellis Island became part of the Statue of Liberty National Monument in 1965.

Between 1892 and 1954, approximately 12 million steerage and third-class steamship passengers were processed and medically checked at Ellis Island. After a multimillion dollar restoration in the mid-1980s, the Main Hall on Ellis Island is now a museum dedicated to the history of immigration to the United States.

Today, in addition to legal immigrants, desperate people still risk their lives to reach the United States illegally. Some seek political freedom; others are desperate for a better economic life. Brave Cubans and Haitians sail on makeshift rafts and boats across the storm-tossed Caribbean Sea to reach Florida. Mexicans eager to find work sneak across the borders of Texas and California. Asian and African stowaways hide in stuffy freighter holds, hoping to make it alive across the ocean.

A U.S. border patrol watches a group of illegal immigrants along an Arizona highway.

When they arrive in the United States, they labor long hours for little pay, usually sending money to their families back home. Illegal immigrants often do not complain about their working conditions because they worry that immigration authorities will find them. After awhile, however, many blend into the general population.

Other visitors, such as students, have visas. These are official documents allowing them to remain in the country until they complete their schooling. If they overstay, they may be deported, or told to leave the country.

The Immigration and Naturalization Service is responsible for tracking all immigrants to the United States. Department workers also check passports of travelers entering the country. After the terrorist attack on New York and Washington, D.C., in 2001, there were plans to divide the service into several parts for better control of the immigrant process.

Anti-Immigrant Attitudes

Immigrants have not always had a warm welcome in the United States. The new arrivals usually spoke a different language, had different customs, and practiced what seemed to be exotic religions. This frightened some people, especially when the newcomers were of a different color or race. The anti-immigrant American Party of the 1850s became known as the Know-Nothings. Whenever they were asked about their attacks on immigrants, they replied, "I know nothing." The Chinese Exclusion Act of 1882 was a deliberate, racist attempt to limit the number of Asians coming to this country.

Even ethnic backgrounds of long-time citizens are occasionally attacked. In the hysteria surrounding World War I, teaching of the German language was forbidden in schools, and German words for common items were made into English. For instance, sauerkraut became "liberty cabbage." Twenty-five years later, Japanese-Americans were imprisoned in camps during World War II because they were considered wartime threats. Despite this, thousands of young Japanese-American men enlisted in the military and earned many awards for their bravery. A park in Waikiki, Hawai'i, is dedicated to these soldiers, sailors, and airmen who served their country so well. Over their long history in America, African Americans also have battled racial attacks and stereotypes. Arab Americans were viewed with suspicion after the terrorist attacks in New York and Washington, D.C., in 2001.

Immigrants Build America

Immigrants have built the United States. Many have moved into jobs that others did not want. They provide a ready pool of labor for factories and service jobs in restaurants and hotels. All these people bring more than just their hands to the United States. They bring their fascinating cultures, ideas, and exceptional talent in many fields. It makes no difference if their name is Boyd, Van Willigenburg, Cortez, Mihelich, Chan, Pesavento, or Triyambakaraj. Each has a gift of self to give to his or her new land.

A Nation Under God

ALTHOUGH THERE IS SEPARATION OF CHURCH AND state in the United States, religion is still reflected at the federal level. Freedom of religion is guaranteed under the First Amendment of the Constitution. The motto "In God We Trust" is found on U.S. currency. The Pledge of Allegiance uses the phrase, "One nation, under God." Visiting temples, mosques, shrines, or churches is important to many families. Even Americans who do not belong to a specific faith or believe in a higher being are generally content to let others worship as they see fit.

The earliest American Indian had a personal kinship with the Great Spirit, a belief that formed the heart of tribal culture. Respect for the earth and its creatures was integral to native traditions. The pounding of a drum meant the heartbeat of life. Young men and women often went on spirit quests, fasted, and yearned for visions that would provide direction for their future. Powerful totem animals and medicine pouches protected them.

From the American colonies' earliest days, spiritual life was considered important. Although church attendance was often required in the small communities of the frontier, North America was a place of spiritual refuge. Fleeing persecution in other countries, religious minorities sought a haven in the New World. Catholics in Maryland, Quakers in Pennsylvania, and Puritans in Massachusetts found safe places to worship as they pleased.

Opposite: **Freedom of religion is granted to all citizens in the United States.**

A Nation Under God **97**

An African American congregation celebrates Sunday mass at the United House of Prayer in New York City.

Americans take advantage of the right to worship whenever, whatever, and wherever they choose. They may participate in mainline denominations or join cults with only a few members. Whatever their basic tenets, or beliefs, these groups provide a moral standard by which to live. These principles are found in the Christian Bible, Muslim Qur'an, Hebrew Talmud, or the Hindu epic poem *Ramayana*. Whether held in an upscale suburb, small rural town, or central city setting, rituals are very important.

Belonging to a faith community is a basic social experience. When a person enters a religious group, it is an excuse for celebration among other members of the community. It is a milestone in life when a young person takes steps toward becoming a grownup, as in Christian confirmation or a Jewish bar or bat mitzvah. The ceremony of marriage is made more special with a blessing by a rabbi, minister, or other clergy.

A thirteen-year-old boy reads from the Torah at his bar mitzvah in front of members of the community of his synagogue.

Religious life in the United States is a complex tapestry of many faiths and philosophies. Some scholars say there are at

Billy Sunday

Preacher Billy Sunday (1862–1935) was a real character. He used his background as a baseball player to liven up his sermons. He would throw off his coat, shout, and wave his arms. People loved his flamboyant presentations and came from miles around to hear him. Born William Sunday in Ames, Iowa, he grew up in an orphanage and went on to play major-league ball through most of the 1880s. Converted while on the circuit, he became a Presbyterian minister in 1903. He supposedly converted, or "saved," 1 million people.

least as many religions as there are residents in the country. They mean that everyone thinks a bit differently about what it means to be religious and how to worship.

The United States does not promote any one religion or a particular form of observance. Therefore, it is very difficult to put a firm figure on the number of people who belong to a particular faith group. Approximately 60 percent of Americans say they belong to an established religious organization, and 70 percent of this figure identify themselves as Christians. The largest denominations in the Christian sphere are Catholics, Baptists, and Methodists.

There is also a growing number of charismatics, or born-agains, such as Pentecostals, who advocate an emotional style of worship. They claim to speak in tongues and to experience visions.

Black Muslim Movement

The Nation of Islam, commonly known as the Black Muslims, was founded by W. D. Fard (1887–1934) in the 1930s. Fard's followers believed he would save African Americans from economic enslavement. Fard was followed by Elijah Muhammad (1897–1975), who continued to combine religious principles with social protest. Muhammad was born Elijah Poole in Sandersville, Georgia. He changed his name when he moved to Detroit in the 1920s. Among his beliefs was that blacks and whites should be separate. Muhammad advocated that part of the United States be set aside for African Americans.

Malcolm X (right), born Malcolm Little in 1925 in Omaha, Nebraska, was a major spokesman of the movement in the 1960s. A powerful orator, he attracted many young African Americans to the cause. He left the Black Muslims in 1964 to embrace traditional Muslim beliefs and was assassinated in 1965.

Elijah Muhammad's son, Warith (Wallace), assumed leadership of the Black Muslims after his father's death and changed its name to the World Community of Islam in the West. Another group, led by Louis Farrakhan, favored keeping the old title and split away. Farrakhan helped organize the Million Man March on Washington on October 16, 1995, to encourage and support African American men as husbands, fathers, and caregivers.

Over the years, preachers have gotten out their message of salvation in many ways. Tent revivals used to bring in crowds eager for rousing hellfire and brimstone sermons. Today, there are even drive-in churches where worshippers sit in their cars while watching the clergy person on a big screen.

Even within mainstream religions, there can be many ideologies, or ways of thinking. Some people are more conservative than others, even within the same organization. This occasionally leads to a schism, or a separation from the main group.

Fastest-Growing Faiths

The Muslim faith is among the fastest-growing religions in the United States, with numbers estimated at about 3 million

One of the fastest-growing religions in the United States is the Muslim faith.

Parochial schools promote teaching academics as well as religious studies.

members, most of whom were born in America. Between 17 to 30 percent of American Muslims are converts. There were about 1,200 mosques in the country in the early 2000s; more than half of these were founded since the 1980s.

Asian religions are also gaining members in the United States, especially as immigrants from Vietnam, Korea, Thailand, Cambodia, and China arrive in greater numbers. Hindus, Buddhists, Taoists, and followers of Confucius bring their own vibrancy of spirit to the religious melting pot that is the United States.

Schools Promote Beliefs

Some religious groups operate private schools for the children of their members. These are called parochial schools. The

Major Religions in the United States

Christian

Roman Catholic	63,000,000
Baptist	36,613,000
Methodist	13,583,000
Pentecostal	10,606,000
Lutheran	8,350,000
Eastern Orthodox	5,302,000
Latter-day Saints	5,100,000
Presbyterian	4,193,000
Churches of Christ	3,500,000
Episcopalian	2,505,000

Non-Christian

Jew	4,300,000
Muslim	3,000,000
Hindu	910,000
Buddhist	780,000
Baha'i	300,000
Chinese folk religions	90,000
Native American	43,000

Roman Catholics have the largest system in the country, with more than 8,000 schools. Non-Catholic schools also have seen a lot of growth since the 1950s. In many communities across the country, Lutherans, Baptists, and Episcopalians have their own schools, as do Jews. In addition to reading, writing, and arithmetic, children in parochial schools study religion and pray regularly.

A number of well-known private universities, such as Harvard, were founded to prepare men for the clergy. Today, these schools admit a broadly diverse range of students, regardless of their religious heritages.

Intolerance Rears Its Head

Religious intolerance in the United States sometimes rears its ugly head due to misinformation or fear. In the nineteenth century, many immigrants did not get jobs because they were Catholic. Although it wasn't stated outright, sometimes Jews were not allowed to join certain country clubs because of their religion. In response, believers combat intolerance though education and court action. For instance, the Anti-Defamation League of B'nai B'rith advocates harmony between Jews and non-Jews. The league is also ready for philosophical or legal battle when necessary.

Church Attendance Dropping

Despite the many people who say they identify with a certain religion, less than half of the U.S. population attends services regularly. This is a worldwide situation, not just affecting the United States. There is also a growing number of the "unchurched," people who do not attend a church at all except for a special event such as a holiday. They may believe in a higher being, but they do not express their faith in a public manner. Others are atheists who do not believe in any god.

Churches still play an important role in the United States,

Religious Calendar

Christmas	December 25
Orthodox Christmas	January 6
Easter	March or April
Passover	March or April
Rosh Hashanah	September
Yom Kippur	September
Ramadan	Ninth month of the Muslim year, usually in late autumn

however. Many churches take the lead in helping the poor and encouraging social justice. The American Friends Service Committee, Baptist Peace Fellowship of North America, Buddhist Peace Fellowship, and Catholic-based Caritas International advocate peaceful resolution of international problems rather than war.

In the 1980s and 1990s, an ecumenical, or worldwide, movement took place. Church groups met to discuss their common beliefs and to review their differences. The Fellowship of Reconciliation and World Council of Churches are among the groups still urging understanding and sharing of values.

Culture and Sport

ANCIENT ARTISTS DREW PETROGLYPHS, OR PICTURES OF animals and hunting scenes, on the walls of caves and on cliff-sides between three to five thousand years ago. Elsewhere in what is now the United States, other long-ago people sculpted mounds in shapes of birds, turtles, and snakes. These shapes, now grass-covered and overgrown by brush, may have marked territory or served as burial sites.

Intricately carved totem poles in the Pacific Northwest were also used for spiritual purposes. Other Indian nations painted their tepees and shield covers, in addition to decorating their garments with beads and shells. Today, American Indian artists such as John Herrera of Laguna Pueblo near Albuquerque, New Mexico, still make beautifully crafted kachina dolls. These traditional figurines are believed by Hopi people to be ancestors of human beings.

Opposite: **Cultural differences vary widely in the United States. These are handmade Indian dolls from New Mexico.**

Settlers Loved Art

The first European settlers, at least the wealthier ones, also enjoyed art. They were eager to have their portraits hanging in their homes. Henrietta Francis Cuthbert and Jeanne MacDonald Lee were two girls whose likenesses were painted in the early 1800s. The paintings now hang in the Abby Aldrich Rockefeller Folk Art Center in Williamsburg, Virginia.

Other artists painted landscapes or religious themes, often in a simplistic, unschooled manner. This is called folk art.

Edward Hicks'
Peaceable Kingdom

Other objects also fall into this category, including weather vanes, toys, business signs, and similar practical items. The Mennello Museum of American Folk Art in Orlando, Florida, showcases works by Edward Hicks (1780–1849) and similar now-famous folk artists.

Toys, Toys, Toys

The evolution of toys followed the development of science and technology in the United States. In colonial days, children played with wooden stick figures and corncob dolls. In more recent times, Raggedy Ann and Andy™, Cabbage Patch Kids®, and Beanie Babies® became popular dolls. The Teddy Bear was named after President Theodore Roosevelt (1858–1919), an ardent outdoorsman, hunter, and environmentalist.

Beanie Babies® had become so popular that McDonald's® began to sell them along with a food purchase.

Barbie® Makes It Big

Barbie®, one of the most famous dolls in the world, was "born" in time for the 1959 American Toy Fair in New York City. Her "mom," Ruth Handler (1916–2002), also founded the Mattel toy company. Handler developed Barbie®, naming the doll after her daughter.

Barbie® evolved from being a model to having a career as a police officer, astronaut, and teacher. Some feminists object to Barbie® as a physical model for girls, yet kids continue to love her. More than 350,000 Barbies were sold in Barbie's first year. Today, more than 1 billion dolls have been sold in 150 countries. In 1961, Ken®, Barbie's "boyfriend," was named after Handler's son. Christie®, an African American doll, came out in 1969.

Toys reflected what was going on in American society. As railroads were being built across the country, toy trains became popular. Some toys had an underlying serious purpose. Erector® sets, Lincoln Logs®, and Tinker Toys® allowed young engineers to build houses and bridges. Chemistry sets encouraged budding scientists. Board games such as Monopoly™ developed business skills.

Famous Literary Figures

Many American writers have made their literary mark on the United States and the world. *Uncle Tom's Cabin* by Harriet Beecher Stowe (1811–1896) caused an upsurge of anti-slavery sentiment in the North before the Civil War. Jack London (1876–1916) was a sailor and adventurer before he wrote such works as *The Call of the Wild* and *White Fang.* F. Scott Fitzgerald (1896–1940) was a gifted novelist and short-story writer whose pieces about the 1920s captured the imagination.

Ernest Hemingway, one of the United States' most well-known writers

Colorful stories by Ernest Hemingway (1899–1961) covered war, bullfighting, and deep-sea fishing. His Pulitzer Prize-winning *The Old Man and the Sea* is as well known today as it was when published in 1952. Nobel Prize-winning writer John Steinbeck (1902–1968) tackled the major social, cultural, and political questions of his day in *The Grapes of Wrath*, *Of Mice and Men*, and other books.

Many notable poets have called the United States their home. Henry Wadsworth Longfellow's (1807–1882) *Evangeline* and "The Wreck of the Hesperus" are often required reading in school. Emily Dickinson (1830–1886), Gertrude Stein (1874–1946), Nikki Giovanni (1943–), and Maya Angelou (1928–) are among the country's best-known women poets.

Well-respected poet, Maya Angelou

Some authors start their careers while they are really young. Susan E. Hinton began her career in high school. She wrote the first draft of *The Outsiders* when she was fifteen. The book, about youth gangs, was published in 1967, when she was seventeen. Hinton's novel sold more than a million copies. Sometimes writing is a group effort. American Indian schoolchildren in Arizona told stories to the author who had them published in 1976 as the book *And It Is Still That Way*.

Growing Up Tough

Award-winning children's author Walter Dean Myers moved to Harlem in New York City from West Virginia after his mother died in 1940. He was three years old at the time. Myers loved to read books even as a child. He had a speech problem that caused him to act up in grade school because he was hard to understand. One teacher suggested he write about himself so that he could deal with his anger. This was a big help, but Myers dropped out of high school to join the army. While in the service, he continued to write and sold some stories to magazines.

Myers entered a contest for African American authors of children's books. Although he had never written for young people before, he won the competition. The editors encouraged him to write more. So he did, turning out wonderfully realistic stories about growing up in the Inner City, life on the streets, jail, and dealing with being a young African American man. Many of his characters play basketball, because he also loved the game. *Bad Boy, Monster, Malcolm X,* and *145th Street: Short Stories* are among Myer's many books.

Media for Reading, Viewing, and Listening

Several major newspapers in the United States are national in scope. Some are very specific in their topics, such as the *The Wall Street Journal*, which covers business. *The New York Times* is considered the national newspaper. Hundreds of weekly newspapers dish up the local scoop to small-town audiences. Chinese, Irish, Polish, and other ethnic readers subscribe to their own newspapers.

Magazines also cater to specialized markets. Dozens of publications aim at the juvenile market. *Soccer Now* and other sports-oriented magazines have devoted fans. Several adult publications also put out juvenile

A newspaper vendor offers a variety of publications for his readers to choose from.

editions, such as *Sports Illustrated for Kids*. Religious organizations also print periodicals such as *Today's Christian Teen*. *New Moon*, published in Duluth, Minnesota, is written and edited by girls eight to fourteen years old. Children also write stories and produce illustrations for *Stone Soup*, a bimonthly magazine out of Santa Cruz, California. Online magazines also cater to young readers.

In addition to ABC, NBC, and CBS, the three national broadcast networks, there are dozens of cable television channels offering history, comedy, music, sports, news, cooking, old movies, or just about any subject a viewer wants. The importance of these targeted new venues was recognized by President Bill Clinton, who regularly appeared on Music Television (MTV). He held "town meetings," chatting with young viewers and even playing his saxophone. These stations are commercial, which means they are supported by advertising.

Public radio and television are kept alive by donations and grants. They broadcast alternative, jazz, or classical music; extended news programs; and cultural shows. Many of these programs are aired from university campuses.

Motion Pictures

The United States is a leader in the film industry, with Universal, Paramount, and MGM studios churning out financial blockbusters such as *Jurassic Park* and *Spiderman*. Hollywood, California, is the center of the American film industry.

Independent filmmakers produce documentaries on serious social issues such as industrial pollution. Some go for more

lighthearted stories on skateboarding or disc jockeys. Independent films winning awards at the annual Sundance Film Festival in Utah are tapped for major release in the nation's theaters. Sundance was started by actor Robert Redford, who encourages new talent in the film industry.

Many child actors become adult performers or move on to interesting new careers in other fields. Shirley Temple was a famous child star in the 1930s. After many film roles, she then went on to be U.S. ambassador to Ghana and Czechoslovakia.

The United States is the leader in film production. Here Sara Jessica Parker is on the set of her film *The Sunshine Boys*.

By the time Haley Joel Osment was 10 years old, he already had numerous film and television roles. He appeared as a haunted little boy in the 1999 movie *The Sixth Sense* and received an Academy Award nomination for his role.

Today, young performers can also get a taste of stage life by appearing in *James and the Giant Peach* or *A Christmas Carol.* Many cities have a children's theater company where beginners can experiment. They then can dream of chasing after the bright lights in New York City's Broadway theater district.

Get the Beat

Rock, grunge, jazz, gospel, classical, ethnic—America has it all when it comes to the beat. Music comes out of life's experience. Frank Sinatra, Perry Como, and Sammy Davis Jr., were velvet-voiced crooners during the good times of the 1950s and 1960s. Woody Guthrie traveled through the 1930s' Depression years, composing and singing folk songs that still carry a punch. Fabled blues artists like Muddy Waters and Leadbelly worked their way up from poverty. Rap is considered to be modern poetry. The lyrics by Jay-Z and Nas are raw and edgy to outsiders, but kids around the world can identify with their songs.

Billboard magazine rates music in many categories. Musicians are excited when their tune makes it to the Top Ten list. *Rolling Stone* and *Downbeat* magazines also cover the music scene.

Popular among U.S. teens, rapper Eminem performs at the 45th Annual Grammy Awards in 2003.

Topping the Charts

Lil' Romeo is one of the youngest artists to make the *Billboard* magazine chart of top hits. He scored in 2001 with his single, "My Baby." Lil' Romeo was eleven years old at the time. His real name is Percy Romeo Miller Jr. and he was born in New Orleans, Louisiana, to a family of famous rappers. Lil' Romeo began making music with his father at age four and was writing his own songs while a straight-A student in fifth grade. When he tours, Lil' Romeo has a tutor to help with his classwork. Even with all this work, he still saves time to watch cartoons and to play basketball.

Athletics are a big business in the United States, with pro players earning millions of dollars a year for their skill. Even amateurs can have a grand time on the course, pitch, diamond, court, or field. Golf, tennis, biking, swimming, darts, ice skating, bowling—you name it and some American is playing it. Americans spend millions of dollars for gear, ranging from soccer balls to football helmets to hockey pads. This enthusiasm spilled over at the 2002 Winter Olympics in Salt Lake City, Utah, when American snowboarders captured the top medals in that exciting first-time competition.

The rest of the world may call it *futbol*, but the sport is still soccer in the United States. Although the game was slow catching on in the United States, tens of thousands of kids and adults now play. They are inspired by World Cup stars such as Mia Hamm. She became the all-time leading scorer in international soccer when she scored her 108 goal in 1999. Hamm was born in 1972 and made the U.S. national team at age fifteen. The men's soccer team earned a spot in the 2002 World Cup matches held in

World Cup soccer star Mia Hamm

Korea and Japan. The matches were watched by an estimated 30 billion television viewers.

American-style football still grabs the most headlines. At Super Bowl parties, fans wait to see which pro team will be the year's champs. Watching the Rose Bowl college football tournament is a New Year's Day holiday tradition. High-school homecoming and state playoff games are always exciting, whether in a large urban area or a small rural community.

Baseball remains the official American pastime. The sport became popular well before the Civil War and is now played around the world. Basketball's popularity has spread through television sports networks. Whether it's hoops star Shaquille O'Neal pounding down the court or kids at the local park, the crowd goes wild over a good slam dunk. Americans love to cheer their sports heroes and heroines.

One of the United States' oldest games, baseball attracts thousands of fans season after season.

Everyday Life in the United States

THERE IS REALLY NO TYPICAL DAY IN THE UNITED STATES. The vast size of the country, the great mix of cultures, and the different home environments affect what children do and how they act. Still, some aspects of life are the same, even if the specifics vary. Most kids go to school, gobble hamburgers, enjoy music, and take in movies. Many play sports, whether going to a skateboard park in Milwaukee, Wisconsin, surfing in Hawai'i, or skiing in Vail, Colorado. Just about all kids love hanging out with their friends. Another great unifying factor is watching television.

Opposite: **Most teens in the United States enjoy hanging out with friends, listening to music, and playing sports.**

"Tag, You're It!"

Tag is an all-around fun game that requires open space and a bunch of friends to play. There are many variations, but elimination tag is the most basic. One player is "it" and tries to tag the other children within a designated area. When a child is tagged, the player is out and has to sit down. The last person to be tagged is "it" for the next game. In Everyone's It, if someone is tagged, they are out of the game. Playing continues until there is one person left. If two players tag each other at the same time, then they are both out. Flag Tag is also fun. Each player tucks the end of his flag into his belt or pants. Others try to pull out the flags to make them "out." The winner is the last one with a flag. In Freeze Tag, one person is "it." When they tag a person, that person has to stand still, or be "frozen."

At the age of sixteen, a U.S. teen is eligible to learn how to drive and attain a driver's license.

The major "rite of passage" into the adult world for kids throughout the United States is passing a driving test at age sixteen or seventeen. Finally getting a license and having access to a vehicle is important because it allows more freedom of movement. There are great distances between friends and social activities in many communities. The United States has become a driving culture. The country uses about 25 percent of the world's energy production, much of which is earmarked for fuel consumption. Half the nation's households have two or more vehicles. Almost 90 percent of all workers in the United States drive to work.

Although school sometimes is a drag, especially on warm, sunny days just before summer vacation, it is a requirement in most states to attend school until age sixteen. There are about 72 million Americans of all ages enrolled in schools through the college level. Of that number, 57 million are in high school or the lower grades. About a million are home-schooled. After grade school, students attend high school. College or trade school often follows.

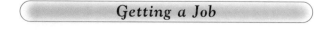

Getting a Job

Trying to get a job is often hard work for U.S. teens because work opportunities are limited. And it is important to have enough education and training to do certain jobs. Regardless of age, however, children who live on farms have plenty of chores to do every day. Before school, they may have to milk the dairy herd, clean horse stalls, help collect eggs, or feed pigs. After school and on weekends, they may need to help mow hay or pull weeds in the family garden. In cities, teens work in fast-food restaurants, for janitorial services, or as hospital aides.

Summer jobs include working for a landscaping company or mowing lawns for neighbors, as well as being a swimming pool lifeguard or a camp counselor. Babysitting is another way American kids earn spending money. Some kids design Web pages and perform other technical tasks.

Most children in the United States live with one or both of their parents, but more and more grandparents live in a household where there are children under eighteen. About 2 million grandparents are responsible for raising their grandchildren because the parents are not in the home for some reason.

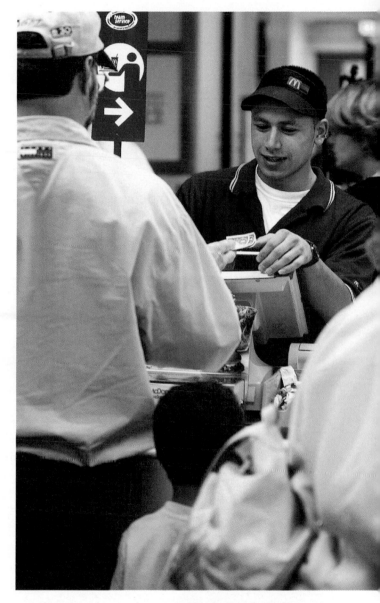

Many teens choose to work at fast food restaurants on weekends and after school.

Of the total population, 253,042,906 persons were born in the United States. Of those, 169,000,000 were born in the state where they currently live. Housing for these people range from mansions in affluent suburbs to tiny city apartments. Unfortunately, sometimes U.S. citizens have been excluded from decent, affordable housing because of their skin color or income. This situation was so bad that the federal government often had to help. The United States Housing Act of 1937 required that the construction of new public housing units be

A housing development in upstate New York was built upon acres of undeveloped land to meet the needs of suburban growth.

matched by the removal of an equal number of run-down dwellings from the local housing supply. In 1968, the Fair Housing Act outlawed any discrimination against people seeking a home.

Today, more than 2.5 million persons live in a one-room house or apartment, while about 9 million have houses with nine or more rooms. The average house has five rooms. After World War II, returning veterans were eager to settle down and raise families. They wanted to escape the closeness of the cities. Developers catered to these wishes and built sprawling suburbs that ate up any land they could purchase.

Holidays in the United States

New Year's Day	January 1
Dr. Martin Luther King Jr. Day	Third Monday in January
Chinese New Year	Second new moon after the beginning of winter
Valentine's Day	February 14
Presidents' Day	Third Monday in February
Arbor Day	April
Earth Day	April 22
Mother's Day	Second Sunday in May
Memorial Day	Last Monday in May
Father's Day	Third Sunday in June
Independence Day	July 4
Labor Day	First Monday in September
Columbus Day	Second Monday in October
Veteran's Day	November
Thanksgiving Day	Fourth Thursday in November
Christmas	December 25
Kwanzaa	December 26

This suburban "Land of No Sidewalks" is very different from the neighborhoods left behind in urban areas. In the 1960s, large tracts of rundown housing were leveled in many cities, and federally subsidized high-rise apartments were built for low-income families. Most of these developments did not work out well, however. Gangs, drugs, and other challenges to family life made these units terrible places in which to raise kids. By the 1990s, many of these facilities were torn down and more secure homes were built. Habitat for Humanity, led by former president Jimmy Carter, is active in building and refurbishing homes for the poor and disadvantaged.

Eating Well

Eating right is relatively easy in the United States, with the abundance of healthy food products. More and more families are trying vegetarian dishes or purchasing organic foods. The United States is not just a melting pot of cultures; it is also a stew pot of tastes. Every ethnic group has its special foods. Some products came from one continent to another and back again. For instance, potatoes were first grown in South America and then were imported to Europe, eventually becoming a staple of Irish diets in the eighteenth and nineteenth centuries. Today, potatoes are grown throughout the United States.

A few common items from America's international menu include tacos, bratwurst, bagels, peanut soup, pickled beets, fry bread, spaghetti, borscht (soup), chow mein, sushi, lefsa (sugared pancakes), and cheese.

An Apple a Day

There are apple fritters, apple dumplings, and all sorts of other recipes made with this delicious fruit. But "mom, the flag, and apple pie" seems to be the phrase that many people think about when they are traveling away from home. The warm scent of a pie brings up many happy memories. While it is easy to purchase a ready-made pie at a store, many people still make their own. There are many variations on making a pie. Here is one to sample, courtesy of http://pie.allrecipes.com

All American Apple Pie

Ingredients

$1\frac{1}{2}$ cups all-purpose flour

$\frac{1}{2}$ cup vegetable oil

2 tablespoons cold milk

$1\frac{1}{2}$ teaspoons white sugar

1 teaspoon salt

6 Fuji apples, cored and sliced

$\frac{3}{4}$ cup white sugar

3 tablespoons all-purpose flour

$\frac{3}{4}$ teaspoon ground cinnamon

$\frac{1}{2}$ teaspoon ground nutmeg

$\frac{1}{2}$ cup all-purpose flour

$\frac{1}{2}$ cup white sugar

$\frac{1}{2}$ cup butter

Directions:

1. Preheat oven to 350°F (175°C).

2. To make crust: In a large bowl, mix together flour, oil, milk, sugar, and salt until evenly blended. Pat mixture into a 9-inch pie pan, spreading the dough evenly over the bottom and up sides. Crimp edges of the dough around the perimeter.

3. To make filling: Mix together 3/4 cup sugar, 3 tablespoons flour, cinnamon, and nutmeg. Sprinkle over apples and toss to coat. Spread evenly in unbaked pie shell.

4. To make topping: Using a pastry cutter, mix together 1/2 cup flour, 1/2 cup sugar, and butter until evenly distributed and crumbly in texture. Sprinkle over apples.

5. Put pie in the oven on a cookie sheet to catch the juices that may spill over. Bake 45 minutes.

Timeline

United States History

American Indians live across what will become the United States.	**c. 15,000 years ago**
Spanish explorer Ponce de Leon lands in St. Augustine, Florida.	A.D. **1513**
English businessmen found Jamestown, Virgina.	**1607**
Plymouth, Massachusetts, is founded.	**1620**
Williamsburg, Virginia, is founded.	**1633**
The Battles of Lexington and Concord take place.	**1775**
The Declaration of Independence is adopted.	**1776**
The Revolutionary War ends with the signing of the Treaty of Paris.	**1783**
An assembly of delegates from the thirteen original colonies meets to draft the Constitution.	**1787**

World History

2500 B.C.	Egyptians build the Pyramids and the Sphinx in Giza.
563 B.C.	The Buddha is born in India.
A.D. **313**	The Roman emperor Constantine recognizes Christianity.
610	The Prophet Muhammad begins preaching a new religion called Islam.
1054	The Eastern (Orthodox) and Western (Roman) Churches break apart.
1066	William the Conqueror defeats the English in the Battle of Hastings.
1095	Pope Urban II proclaims the First Crusade.
1215	King John seals the Magna Carta.
1300s	The Renaissance begins in Italy.
1347	The Black Death sweeps through Europe.
1453	Ottoman Turks capture Constantinople, conquering the Byzantine Empire.
1492	Columbus arrives in North America.
1500s	The Reformation leads to the birth of Protestantism.
1776	The Declaration of Independence is signed.
1789	The French Revolution begins.

United States History

The Louisiana Purchase doubles the size of United States.	1803
The United States defeats Mexico and acquires more territory in the Southwest and in California.	1845
Confederate states secede from the Union, and the Civil War begins.	1861
The Civil War ends with the defeat of the Confederacy.	1865
The Spanish American War concludes with a U.S. victory.	1898
Congress declares war on the German Empire.	1917
The armistice is signed, ending World War I.	1918
Women gain the right to vote with ratification of the 19th Amendment.	1920
The stock market crashes.	1929
The United States enters World War II when the Japanese attack Pearl Harbor.	1941
The United States becomes involved in Vietnam, to be caught up in the longest war in its history.	1957
President John F. Kennedy is assassinated.	1963
The Gulf War is launched to drive Iraq from oil-rich Kuwait.	1990
U.S troops and allies pursue al-Qaeda terrorists in Afghanistan.	2002
The United States goes to war with Iraq.	2003

World History

1865	The American Civil War ends.
1914	World War I breaks out.
1917	The Bolshevik Revolution brings communism to Russia.
1929	Worldwide economic depression begins.
1939	World War II begins, following the German invasion of Poland.
1945	World War II ends.
1957	The Vietnam War starts.
1969	Humans land on the moon.
1975	The Vietnam War ends.
1979	Soviet Union invades Afghanistan.
1983	Drought and famine in Africa.
1989	The Berlin Wall is torn down, as communism crumbles in Eastern Europe.
1991	Soviet Union breaks into separate states.
1992	Bill Clinton is elected U.S. president.
2000	George W. Bush is elected U.S. president.
2001	Terrorists attack World Trade Towers, New York and the Pentagon, Washington, D.C.

Fast Facts

Official name: United States of America

Capital: Washington, D.C.

Official language: None, but English is predominant

The flag of the United States

Grand Canyon

Official religion:	None
Year of founding:	Declaration of Independence adopted, July 4, 1776; Constitution ratified, September 17, 1787
National anthem:	"The Star-Spangled Banner," written by Francis Scott Key
Government:	Federal republic
Chief of state:	President
Area:	4 million square miles (10 million sq km); mainland United States is 2,807 miles (4,517 km) from east to west and 1,200 miles (1,930 km) from north to south
Latitude and longitude of geographic center:	Lower forty-eight states—4 miles (6.4 m) west of Lebanon, Kansas Longitude: 98° 35' west Latitude: 39° 50' north All fifty states (including Hawai'i and Alaska)—17 miles (27.3 m) west of Castle Rock, South Dakota Latitude: 44° 58' north Longitude: 103° 46' west
Highest elevation:	Mount McKinley, Alaska, 20,320 feet (6,198 m)
Lowest elevation:	Death Valley, California, 282 feet (86 m) below sea level
Average temperatures:	January, -7°F to 75°F (-21°C to 23°C); July, 45°F to 106°F (70°C to 41°C)
Average annual rainfall (contiguous states):	7.53 inches (19.1 cm) to 72.1 inches (183.2 cm)

Statue of Liberty

Currency

National population (2000 census):	281,421,906	
Population of largest cities (2000 census):	New York City	8,008,278
	Los Angeles	3,694,820
	Chicago	2,896,016
	Houston	1,953,631
	Philadelphia	1,517,550

Famous landmarks:
▶ *The White House,* Washington, D.C.

▶ *Lincoln Memorial,* Washington, D.C.

▶ *Vietnam Veterans Memorial,* Washington, D.C.

▶ *Statue of Liberty,* New York City

▶ *Grand Canyon,* Arizona

▶ *Great Lakes,* United States–Canada border

Industry: The country manufactures everything from automobiles to nuts and bolts. It exports both raw materials and finished goods to markets around the world. There is also a large service industry in the health, financial, and communications fields.

Currency: One hundred cents make one dollar, the basic unit of American currency. There are $1, $2, $5, $10, $20, $50, $100, and $1,000 bills. Coins include the penny, nickel, dime, quarter, half-dollar, and dollar.

Weights and measures: The United States uses the common system of measurement.

Literacy rate: 97 percent

132 *United States of America*

Game of tag

Common words and phrases:

Burn the candle at both ends	Work too hard
Bust a gut	Work harder
Get the lead out	Go fast
Go to pot	Become a failure
Fast as greased lightning	Go faster
Hold your horses	Slow down
In the nick of time	Just in time
In the groove	Have a good, fun spirit
Keep under your hat	Keep a secret
Jump the gun	Start too soon
Like a bull in a china shop	Clumsy
More than one way to skin a cat	More than one way to do something

Famous Americans:

Maya Angelou   (1928–)
Poet

Frederick Douglass   (1818–1895)
African American activist, diplomat, presidential consultant

Ernest Hemingway   (1899–1961)
Author, sportsman

Abraham Lincoln   (1809–1865)
Sixteenth president, U.S. leader during American Civil War

Sitting Bull   (c. 1834–1890)
American Indian leader

Elizabeth Cady Stanton   (1815–1902)
Women's rights advocate

George Washington   (1732–1799)
First president, Revolutionary War hero

Sitting Bull

To Find Out More

Nonfiction

▶ Cheney, Lynn V. *America: A Patriotic Primer*. New York: Simon & Schuster, 2002.

▶ Foner, Eric, and Garrarty, John A., ed. *The Reader's Companion to American History*. Boston: Houghton Mifflin, 1991.

▶ Hakim, Joy. *History of the U.S.* (11 volume set). Cary, N.C.: Oxford University Press, 1999.

▶ Hoose, Phillip. *We Were There, Too: Young People in U.S. History*. New York: Farrar Straus & Giroux, 2001.

▶ Houston, Jeanne Wakatsuki, and Houston, James D. *Farewell to Manzanar: A True Story of Japanese American Experience During and After World War II Internment*. Westminster, Md.: Bantam Books, 1983.

▶ Johnson, James E., and Kavanagh, Jack. *The Irish in America*. Minneapolis: Lerner, 1994.

▶ Johnston, Robert. *The Making of America: The History of the United States from 1492 to the Present*. Washington, D.C.: National Geographic, 2002.

▶ Maxwell, James, ed. *America's Fascinating Indian Heritage*. Pleasantville, N.Y.: The Reader's Digest Association, 1990.

▶ Snell, Tee Loftin. *The Wild Shores: America's Beginnings*. Washington, D.C.: The National Geographic Society, 1974.

▶ Stanley, Jerry. *Children of the Dust Bowl: The True Story of the School at Weedpatch Camp*. Westminster, Md.: Crown Publishing, 1993.

▶ Tanaka Shelley. *Attack on Pearl Harbor: The True Story of the Day America Entered World War II*. New York: Hyperion Press, 2001.

▶ Warren, Robert Penn. *Remember the Alamo!* New York: Random House, 1958.

▶ Webb, Robert N. *We Were There at the Boston Tea Party*. New York: Grosset & Dunlap, 1956.

Fiction

▶ Emerson, Kathy Lynn. *Julia's Mending*. New York: Orchard Books, 1987.

▶ Keith, Harold. *Rifle for Watie*. Scranton, Pa: Harper Trophy, 1989.

▶ Paulsen, Gary. *The Crossing*. New York: Orchard Books, 1987.

Biography

▶ Hintz, Martin. *Wisconsin Portraits: 55 People Who Made a Difference*. Black Earth, Wis.: Trails Books, 2000.

▶ Jackson, George F. *Black Women Makers of History: A Portrait*. Oakland, Calif.: GRT Publishing, 1975.

▶ Novas, Himilce. *The Hispanic 100. A Ranking of the Latino Men and Women Who Have Most Influenced American Thought and Culture*. New York: Citadel Press, 1995.

Web Sites

▶ **Berite's Best Sites for Children**
http://www.beritsbest.com
For homework help in science, arts, and health.

▶ **Ben's Guide**
http://bensguide.gpo.gov
Provides details on the meaning of citizenship and how to become a citizen.

▶ **Fact Monster**
http://www.factmonster.com
For help with news, United States history, sports, and science.

Organizations

▶ **National Park Service**
http://www.nps.gov

▶ **U.S. Census Bureau**
United States Department of Commerce
Washington, D.C. 20230
http://www.census.gov

▶ **U.S. Weather Research Center**
3227 Audley St.
Houston, TX 77098

▶ **The White House**
www.whitehousekids.gov

Index

Page numbers in *italics* indicate illustrations.

Meet the Author

MARTIN HINTZ has written numerous books for Children's Press and other publishers. He has traveled extensively around the United States to write stories for newspapers and magazines and has produced a number of guidebooks. For his assignments over a thirty-year journalism career, he toured galleries and factories, drove over mountain passes and along superhighways, hiked trails and walked through large cities, swam in the Pacific Ocean and splashed in the Atlantic. Hintz has visited almost every state for his work. He was born in Iowa and now lives in Milwaukee, Wisconsin, with his wife, Pam Percy, a radio producer and author.

Hintz's research for this book included visiting the local library to find books on U.S. history and culture. He also found that surfing the Internet was very helpful in researching facts.

Hintz is a past president and board chairman of the Society of American Travel Writers and belongs to the Society of Professional Journalists and several other journalism associations.

Just like many other Americans, Hintz has a mixed heritage. He is half German, one-quarter Irish, and one-quarter Norwegian. His ancestors have been American citizens since the 1850s.

Photo Credits